SHORTLIST

Istanbul

WHAT'S NEW | WHAT'S ON | WHAT'S BEST

www.timeout.com/istanbul

Contents

Istanbul by Area

Essentials

Published by Time Out Guides Ltd
Universal House
251 Tottenham Court Road
London W1T 7AB
Tel: + 44 (0)20 7813 3000
Fax: + 44 (0)20 7813 6001
Email: guides@timeout.com
www.timeout.com

Managing Director Peter Fiennes
Editorial Director Ruth Jarvis
Business Manager Daniel Allen
Editorial Manager Holly Pick
Assistant Management Accountant Ija Krasnikova

Time Out Guides is a wholly owned subsidiary of Time Out Group Ltd.

© **Time Out Group Ltd**
Director & Founder Tony Elliott
Chief Executive Officer David King
Group Financial Director Paul Rakkar
Group General Manager/Director Nichola Coulthard
Time Out Communications Ltd MD David Pepper
Time Out International Ltd MD Cathy Runciman
Time Out Magazine Ltd Publisher/Managing Director Mark Elliott
Group Commercial Director Graeme Tottle
Production Director Mark Lamond
Group IT Director Simon Chappell

Time Out and the Time Out logo are trademarks of Time Out Group Ltd.

This edition first published in Great Britain in 2010 by Ebury Publishing
A Random House Group Company
Company information can be found on www.randomhouse.co.uk
Random House UK Limited Reg. No. 954009
10 9 8 7 6 5 4 3 2 1

Distributed in the US and Latin America by Publishers Group West (1-510-809-3700)
Distributed in Canada by Publishers Group Canada (1-800-747-8147)

For further distribution details, see www.timeout.com

ISBN: details 978-1-84670-089-7

A CIP catalogue record for this book is available from the British Library.

Printed and bound in Germany by Appl.

The Random House Group Limited supports The Forest Stewardship Council (FSC), the leading
international forest certification organisation. All our titles that are printed on Greenpeace
approved FSC certified paper carry the FSC logo. Our paper procurement policy can be found
at www.rbooks.co.uk/environment.

Time Out carbon-offsets all its flights with Trees for Cities (www.treesforcities.org).

Istanbul Shortlist

The **Time Out Istanbul Shortlist** is one of a new series of guides that draws on Time Out's background as a magazine publisher to keep you current with what's going on in town. As well as Istanbul's key sights and the best of its eating, drinking and leisure options, the guide picks out the most exciting venues to have recently opened and gives a full calendar of annual events. It also includes features on the important news, trends and openings, all compiled by locally based editors and writers. Whether you're visiting for the first time, or you're a regular, you'll find the *Time Out Istanbul Shortlist* contains all you need to know, in a portable and easy-to-use format.

The guide divides central Istanbul into two areas, each of which contains listings for Sights & Museums, Eating & Drinking, Shopping, Nightlife and Arts & Leisure, with maps pinpointing all their locations. At the front of the book are chapters rounding up these scenes city-wide, and giving a shortlist of our overall picks in a variety of categories. We include itineraries for days out, plus essentials such as transport information and hotels.

Istanbul's districts have different area codes: 0212 for Europe; 0216 for Asia. You need use these codes only if dialling from the opposite shore, or from elsewhere in Turkey. The country code for Turkey is 90. To call from outside Turkey follow this with the number given, dropping the initial '0'.

We have noted price categories by using one to four US dollar signs ($-$$$$), representing budget, moderate, expensive and luxury. Major credit cards are accepted unless otherwise stated. We also indicated when a venue is NEW.

All our listings are double-checked, but places do close or change their hours or prices, so it's a good idea to call a venue before visiting. While every effort has been made to ensure accuracy, the publishers cannot accept responsibility for any errors that this guide may contain.

Venues are marked on the maps using symbols numbered according to their order within the chapter and colour-coded according to the type of venue they represent:

❶ Sights & Museums
❶ Eating & Drinking
❶ Shopping
❶ Nightlife
❶ Arts & Leisure

Map key	
Major sight or landmark	
Hospital or college	
Railway station	
Parks	
River	
Motorway	
Main road	
Main road tunnel	
Pedestrian road	
Steps	
City Wall	—
Tram	—●—
Airport	✈
Church	✚
Mosque	☪
Metro station	Ⓜ
Area name	FATIH

Time Out **Istanbul** Shortlist

EDITORIAL
Editor Daniel Neilson
Deputy Editor Ros Sales
Proofreader Sally Davies

DESIGN
Art Director Scott Moore
Art Editor Pinelope Kourmouzoglou
Senior Designer Kei Ishimaru
Group Commercial Designer Jodi Sher

Picture Editor Jael Marschner
Acting Deputy Picture Editor Liz Leahy
Picture Desk Assistant/Researcher
Ben Rowe

ADVERTISING
New Business & Commercial Director
Mark Phillips

International Advertising Manager
Kasimir Berger
International Sales Executive Charlie Sokol
Advertising Sales (Istanbul)
Time Out Istanbul

MARKETING
**Sales & Marketing Director, North America
& Latin America** Lisa Levinson
Senior Publishing Brand Manager
Luthfa Begum
Group Commercial Art Director
Anthony Huggins
Marketing Co-ordinator Alana Benton

PRODUCTION
Production Manager Brendan McKeown
Production Controller Katie Mulhern

CONTRIBUTORS
This guide was researched and written by Daniel Neilson and the writers of
Time Out Istanbul.

PHOTOGRAPHY
Photography by Fumie Suzuki; except pages 8, 13, 14, 17, 20, 73, 84, 88, 110
Daniel Neilson.

The following images were provided by the featured establishments/artists: pages 7,
26, 29, 31, 32, 34, 35, 107, 133, 134, 137, 140, 143, 145, 146, 149.

Cover image: Sultanahmet (Blue) Mosque.
Credit: Photolibrary.com.

MAPS
JS Graphics (john@jsgraphics.co.uk).

About **Time Out**

Founded in 1968, Time Out has expanded from humble London beginnings into the
leading resource for those wanting to know what's happening in the world's greatest
cities. As well as our influential what's-on weeklies in London, New York and Chicago,
we publish nearly 30 other listings magazines in cities as varied as Beijing and Mumbai.
The magazines established Time Out's trademark style: sharp writing, informed
reviewing and bang up-to-date inside knowledge of every scene.

Time Out made the natural leap into travel guides in the 1980s with the City Guide
series, which now extends to over 50 destinations around the world. Written and
researched by expert local writers and generously illustrated with original photography,
the full-size guides cover a larger area than our Shortlist guides and include many more
venue reviews, along with additional background features and a full set of maps.

Throughout this rapid growth, the company has remained proudly independent,
still owned by Tony Elliott four decades after he started Time Out London as a single
fold-out sheet of A5 paper. This independence extends to the editorial content of all
our publications, this Shortlist included. No establishment has been featured because
it has advertised, and no payment has influenced any of our reviews. And, for our critics,
there's definitely no such thing as a free lunch: all restaurants and bars are visited and
reviewed anonymously, and Time Out always picks up the bill.
For more about the company, see www.timeout.com.

Don't Miss

Topkapı Palace p49

Sights & Museums

The city of Istanbul is a living museum. Turn a corner and you'll find a vista on to an ancient, exciting and tumultuous past. The tales of power, trade and immigration can be seen in the city's skyline, which has some of the world's most interesting and distinctive architecture.

But for one geographical quirk, the Bosphorus, Istanbul as we know it would not exist. The strait that links the Black Sea – and Russia, Georgia, Ukraine, Georgia, Bulgaria and Romania – with the Sea of Marmara, and consequently the Aegean Sea and the Mediterranean, has meant that Istanbul has, for more than 3,000 years, been located on one of the globe's most important strategic positions, between the continents of Europe and Asia.

The Bosphorus & Golden Horn

Istanbul lives on the Bosphorus. It is focused on its waterway in a way that is no longer true for Paris, London or New York. And it's not just used for pleasure cruises: commuter ferries and fishing boats, cargo ships and oil tankers ply these waters. For the visitor, it's quicker, and much more pleasant, to navigate coastal Istanbul by passenger ferry than by road.

The waterways also divide the city. The two key areas we have used in this guide are north and south of the Golden Horn. The Golden Horn is a seven kilometre-long inlet that separates Old Istanbul – the Istanbul of domes and minarets – and new Istanbul, the Istanbul of bars and restaurants, the Istanbul of the Republic. Most of the sights and museums are south of the Golden Horn, especially in the neighbourhoods of Sultanahmet, Eminönü and the Bazaar Quarter. However, over the Galata Bridge and into Beyoğlu is where most visitors spend their evenings.

South of the Golden Horn

The Süleymaniye Mosque (see p70), built by Süleyman the Magnificent's master architect, Mimar Sinan, in 1577, is the most spectacular and commanding of the many mosques on the skyline south of the Golden Horn. The Sultanahmet (Blue) Mosque (see p59), distinctive for its six minarets (a controversial addition because it was said that only the mosque of Mecca should have six minarets), is a pretender to Sinan's masterpiece and a less successful construction, although the interior tile work, in the blue Iznik style that gives the mosque its name, is highly accomplished.

Administrative hub of the Ottoman Empire and home to its sultans for many years, the vast Topkapı Palace (see p49), occupies much of the tip of the peninsula of old Istanbul. A full day is needed to explore the four courts of the complex, one following another and housing increasingly important members of the sultan's entourage. The harem is a highlight of any visit, as is the imperial treasury. Beside the palace grounds is the Archaeology Museum (see p53), home to relics from pre-Roman times, and from the Byzantine and Ottoman eras.

Just outside Topkapı Palace is Haghia Sophia (see p54), instantly recognisable from its majestic dome. The Roman Emperor Justinian dedicated the church in AD 537, and its dome

SHORTLIST

Unmissable sights
- Grand Bazaar (see p65)
- Haghia Sophia (see p54)
- Topkapı Palace (see p49)

Most educational
- Atatürk Museum (see p122)
- Archaeology Museum (see p53)
- Jewish Museum (see p116)
- Military Museum (see p122)

Quirkiest museums
- Galatasaray Museum (see p94)
- Rahmi M Koç Museum (see p122)
- Sakıp Sabancı Museum (see p128)

Best for modern art
- Istanbul Modern (see p115)
- SantralIstanbul (see p118)

Best for traditional art
- Mimar Sinan University Museum of Fine Arts (see p126)
- Museum of Turkish & Islamic Art (see p58)

Beautiful mosques
- Küçük Haghia Sophia Mosque (see p56)
- New Mosque (see p72)
- Rustem Paşa Mosque (see p72)
- Sokollu Mehmet Paşa Mosque (see p58)

Ancient history
- Egyptian obelisk (see p54)
- Hippdrome (see p54)

Best views
- Galata Tower (see p79)
- Süleymaniye Mosque (see p70)

TimeOut

timeout.com/travel
Get the local experience

Camel racing in the United Arab Emirates

©Bernardino Testa/ITP Images

took on an almost fabled status, said to glow at night like a great golden beacon. In 1317, however, a series of ugly buttresses was deemed necessary when the church seemed in danger of collapse. Ransacked by Western crusaders in 1204, it became a mosque after the Ottoman Turks breached the city walls in 1453. Today, it's a designated museum – a move by the secular Republic in the 1930s that remains controversial today. Aside from the size and shape of its interior, its other extraordinary feature are its Byzantine mosaics.

These sights can get very busy, so it's best to visit as early as possible.

There are a number of other places of interest in the area that are often overlooked. The Museum of Turkish and Islamic Art (see p58) offers an insight into the history of the neighbourhood, and its impressive artistic heritage. Küçük Haghia Sophia Mosque (see p56), 'Little Haghia Sophia', has a fine frieze honouring Emperor Justinian. And down by Galata Bridge is the New Mosque

(see p72), completed in 1663, and the Rüstem Paşa Mosque (see p72), one of Sinan's masterpieces, but often overlooked by visitors.

One of the loveliest, and quietest, areas south of the Golden Horn is Beyazıt Square. On the plaza, in front of a monumental gate leading in to the Istanbul University campus, is the busy Beyazıt Mosque. Once here, take a deep breath before descending into the maze of the Grand Bazaar – the world's oldest shopping centre. The animated, cajoling shopkeepers can make the network of alleyways and vaulted passages seem even more bewildering. Sadly, much of the Grand Bazaar, especially the main thoroughfares, is aimed squarely at tourists; better to get lost among the side alleys to see where Istanbullus still shop.

North of the Golden Horn

Galata Bridge, which crosses the Golden Horn, is one of the liveliest places in Istanbul. As well as being a principal crossing for cars and trams – the quickest way to get

Grand Bazaar

from one area to the other – it's popular with pedestrians, who like to stop and admire the view, and fishermen. Anchovies are pulled up in their thousands, many cooked on makeshift barbecues or sold to the fish stalls that spread along both sides of the bridge.

Beyoğlu is an all-encompassing term for the older neighbourhoods of Galata, Tünel, Pera, Çukurcuma and Cihangir, extending up towards Taksim Square. It's the centre of modern, secular Istanbul. Its main thoroughfare is the pedestrianised Istiklal Caddesi, which, since the birth of the modern republic in 1923, is where Istanbullus go to shop, socialise and be seen. Many buildings date from the 19th century, but it's the 14th-century Galata Tower (see p79) that is the main landmark. It's possible to climb the circular watchtower; there are panoramic views over the Bosphorus and Sultanahmet from the top.

Beyoğlu is the city's cultural centre. Private art and photography galleries line Istiklal Caddesi (see p94). Parallel is upmarket Meşrutiyet Caddesi and the Pera Museum. This gallery has a good collection dating from the 17th to 19th centuries, and its temporary exhibition roster gets better all the time, attracting blockbusters from artists such as Fernando Botero.

Nearby the Pera Palace (see p142), Istanbul's most famous hotel, is significant for its architecture and position as the destination of passengers after stepping off the Orient Express. It provided clean sheets and fluffy pillows for Agatha Christie, who wrote part of *Murder on the Orient Express* in room 411. Atatürk's room, meanwhile, has been kept as it was when he stayed here regularly.

In the 19th and early 20th centuries, Galata and Pera were wealthy, influential and influenced by European style; it was only natural that they should import international architectural fashions. the city's art nouveau heritage is visible in buildings across the area, with a fine example of the style of the era at the Botter House (Istiklal Caddesi 475-7).

Beyoğlu becomes brutal at Taksim Square, an ugly central traffic-choked plaza. Of importance is the Independence Monument celebrating Mustafa Kemal Atatürk's declaration of a new republic in 1923.

Art by the sea

Further down by the Bosphorus are two of Istanbul's finest galleries. Istanbul Modern (see p115), opened in 2004, is invaluable for an overview of Turkish art in the last 100 years. The Mimar Sinan University Museum of Fine Arts (see p126) has some excellent (and older) pieces too, including works by Osman Hamdi Bey.

Beyond the centre

Although visitors rarely stray beyond Sultanahmet and Beyoğlu, there are some fine sights and museums further out of town. Just by the Fatih Mehmet Bridge, is Rumeli Hisarı fortress (see p126). The three imposing towers and defensive walls were built in the 14th century as part of Mehmet II's master plan to capture Constantinople. In stark contrast is the Sakıp Sabancı Museum, housed in a fine villa built in 1920. Many of the rooms still have their original furnishings (the villa belonged to Egyptian royalty), but the museum is primarily known for its calligraphy exhibits. There's also a fine restaurant: Müzedechanga (see p131).

House Café p129

WHAT'S BEST

Eating & Drinking

Until recently, Istanbul's culinary options were long on tradition but short on innovation. The meze, a shared feast of hot and cold dishes washed down with lots of the anis-flavoured spirit rakı, is still the city's favourite meal and looks as if it will remain so. Meze is consistently delicious, but the *meyhanes* (tavernas) where it is traditionally served are often as much about socialising (and drinking, singing and dancing) as about food. *Meyhanes* are where Istanbullus go to let their hair down.

However, over the past few years, a number of internationally renowned chefs of Turkish origin have returned home to reinvent Anatolian cuisine, using techniques they've picked up in Parisian bistros, New York restaurants and British gastropubs. This has led to a surge in fine dining restaurants around the city. Some of the new batch are examples of style over substance, but the best, listed in this book, fuse (in the best possible way) exceptional cooking and seasonal ingredients in well-designed dining rooms and with quality service.

Meze meals

Walk down Nevizade Sokak in Beyoğlu on any given evening of the week, and the number of diners packing into the *meyhanes* is astonishing. Istanbullus love to eat out. An evening in a *meyhane*, animatedly discussing the topics of the day, while eating a great array of dishes, and, once the evening gets going, belting out a few folk songs, is a joyous way

Cuppa p112

to spend an evening. The city's most famous *meyhane* district is the Çiçek Pasajı, an elegant 19th-century arcade off Istiklal Caddesi. However, locals prefer neighbouring Nevizade Sokak, an alley lined with restaurants leading off Balık Pazarı (Fish Market).

There are dozens of restaurants, and they don't differ much in terms of price and quality. We like Krependeki Imroz (see p101). Founded in 1941, it's one of the oldest *meyhanes* in the city and has good food, friendly waiters and reasonable prices. Boncuk (see p100) specialises in Armenian dishes, while Cumhuriyet Meyhanesi (see p100), once frequented by Atatürk, is notable for its *fasıl* musicians. For quality fish, try Mer Balık (see p101).

Cold dishes cost around YTL8, hot ones YTL6-YTL15, and seafood appetisers YTL10-YTL25. For two people, six dishes are usually enough; you can order main courses later if you have room.

Vegetarians should be able to find plenty to eat from the meze choices, although *meyhanes* won't be able to vouch for totally animal produce free ingredients. To ensure completely meat-free meals, you'll need to go to a different kind of restaurant: try Nature and Peace (see p104) or Zencefil (see p105).

Shooting stars

At the end of 2009, Murat Bozok opened Mimolett (see p103) with the express intention of bringing the first Michelin star to Turkey. His CV is certainly promising – past posts have included head chef at Gordon's Ramsay's Devonshire and spells with Alain Ducasse, Pierre Gagnaire and Joel Robuchon. His cooking is a fusion of Turkish food with modern French techniques, and it's fabulous.

Some see Mimolett (and the high prices of food of this kind) as a risk in Istanbul. But it was a calculated risk. Mimolett joins the ranks of restaurants such as Mikla (see p91). With chef Mehmet Gurs at the helm, Mikla offers a successful fusion menu of Turkish and Scandinavian ingredients and styles. Its location, in the roof garden of the 18-storey Marmara Pera hotel, is commanding. The view from Topaz (see p104) is equally spectacular and the food on a par. Topaz offers two menus – the first takes traditional Ottoman cuisine to its highest levels, while the innovative Mediterranean menu offers a broader range of styles and uses more modern techniques. Leb-i Derya Richmond (see p96), at the top of the Richmond Hotel, probably has the best view of all Istanbul restaurants, along with a fine menu.

Elsewhere, other hotel restaurants also win praise. Both of the Four Seasons hotels (see p62 and p148) serve good Mediterranean food. The Çırağan Palace Kempinski (see p148) is home to the upmarket Tuğra. And the best steak house in Istanbul is undoubtedly the Prime at the new Park Hyatt Maçka Palas hotel (see p147).

Fresh fish

Istanbul is where the Bosphorus links the Black Sea to the Sea of Marmara and the Aegean. Some say that it's this meeting of many waters that is responsible for the great variety of seafood found here. You'll often find the catch of the day scrawled on a whiteboard in restaurants in Kumkapı, south of the Golden Horn. A network of streets here is home to more than 40 fish restaurants, some better than others (and it isn't always easy to tell). Our pick of the bunch is Çapari (see p65) and Akvaryum Fish Restaurant (see p65) – but if in doubt, head to the one that's busiest with locals. Over in Sultanahmet, meanwhile, the finest seafood restaurant is the often-overlooked Balıkçı Sabahattin (see p61).

On the street

Despite all the upmarket eateries, it's still the case that some of Istanbul's best food can be found on the street. Kebabs here are a far cry from the sad post-pub doners found in Britain; these have good meat and fresh bread. Kebab stalls are

SHORTLIST

Fine dining
- Mikla (see p91)
- Mimolett (see p103)
- Topaz (see p104)

Rooms with a view
- 360 (see p95)
- Beşinci Kat (5.Kat) (see p112)
- Leb-I Deyra Richmond (see p96)

For design lovers
- Kitchenette (see p103)
- House Café (see p129)
- Lokal (see p85)
- Müzedechanga (see p131)

For fish
- Akvaryum Fish Restaurant (see p65)
- Balıkçı Sabahattin (p61)
- Doğa Balık (see p112)

Veg out
- Nature and Peace (see p104)
- Zencefil (see p105)

For Ottoman classics
- Asitane (see p121)
- Mozaik (see p62)

For simple snacks
- Canim Ciğerim (see p79)
- Hamdi Et Lokantası (see p75)

Best meyhanes
- Cumhuriyet Meyhanesi (see p100)
- Krependeki Imroz (see p101)
- Refik (see p86)

Best for a beer
- Badehane (see p79)
- Enginar (see p85)

Coffee break
- Cuppa (see p112)
- Smyrna (see p114)

everywhere; try the ones along Bal Pazari by Nevizade Sokak. There's also great, fresh fast food from the sea. Along the Bosphorus and around the Galata Bridge are stalls (and bobbing boats) selling fish sandwiches made from the day's catch. There are also makeshift restaurants where, for a few lira, you'll be served a plate of fried anchovies, fresh bread and a small salad. Try Iskele Balik (see p85).

A favourite among Istanbullus is *kokoreç* – grilled intestines, chopped with vegetables and herbs and served in fresh bread. Stalls can be found across Istanbul – look for the horizontal skewer wrapped with an intestine, above a flame . Although not for the squeamish, they're delicious. Try the stalls along Galip Dede Caddesi.

Then there's the Anatolian dish of goat's head. The city's most famous seller of this delicacy is to be found along Balık Pazari – he'll open up the head, pulling out the tasty tongue and other bits of meat, and serve it with parsley, garlic and spices.

Café culture

Coffee-drinking has a long heritage here. Sadly, Starbucks seems to have taken over from old-style coffee houses in upmarket neighbourhoods, but you can also find some great independent western-style cafés. The House Café (see p129), which has 11 branches across the city, offers great coffee, excellent food and some of the city's most stylish interiors. Other good places to while away the afternoon include Kaktüs (see p96), Cuppa (see p112) and Café Ara (see p95).

Drinking

The city's best drinking establishments are around Beyoğlu. In summer, the pavements around

Tünel fill up from 5pm everyday with groups knocking back beers and chewing on nuts. Perennial favourites include KV Café (see p85) and Badehane (see p79), which is also great for live gypsy music. Many bars are masters in retro design style. This is particularly true around the city's hippest neighbourhood, Cihangir. Meyra (see p112) and Smyrna (see p114) are both styled this way, and filled with top-tapping writers and couples enjoying relaxed afternoons.

There isn't a huge number of places in Istanbul to enjoy an expertly mixed cocktail, but often the best are to be found where there are the best views. Leb-I Deyra Richmond (see p96), 5.Kat (see p112) and Nu Teras (see p91) area all rooftop bars with superb panoramas over the city.

Beyond the centre

Beyoğlu doesn't quite have the monopoly on the best eating and drinking. Along the trendy Bosphorus villages is one of the finest new additions to Istanbul's culinary scene, Abracadabra (Arnavutköy Caddesi 50, 0212 358 6087, www.abracadabra-ist.com). Chef Dilara Erbay has travelled the country uncovering original recipes and sourcing the finest ingredients. Müzedechanga (see p131), in the Sakıp Sabancı Museum in Emirgan is also well regarded, and the setting overlooking the Bosphorus is delightful.

One of our favourite restaurants in Istanbul is over on the Asian shore. Ciya (see box p129) is an unassuming place in Kadıköy, but the food is exceptional (there's no alcohol). It serves classic Anatolian dishes, but somehow they taste better than anywhere else in the city.

The Works: Objects of Desire p111

WHAT'S BEST
Shopping

Istanbul is, of course, the site of the world's first shopping centre: the Grand Bazaar. For more than half a millennium, this rabbit warren of vaulted passageways was the principal trading post of the Ottoman Empire. It's where traders from Yemen, Anatolia, the Balkans and Middle East traded spices and textiles, soaps and animals.

For better or worse, the Grand Bazaar in the 21st century is mostly given over to tourism. Jewellery, souvenirs and rugs are all hawked to foreign visitors. Some old customs still hold sway, though: you are still expected to bargain for your purchase, and many shop oweners still pay their annual rent in gold.

Much of the shopping experiences in Istanbul take place in that modern version of the bazaar: the shopping mall.

Globalisation in the world of retail means that Istanbullus can now cruise Harvey Nichols, snack on noodles at Wagamama and then stock up on Häagen-Dazs. Newer centres such as Kanyon (see p124) and, in particular, Istinye Park (Istinye Bayıddesi 185, Levent www.istinyepark.com), are unashamedly upmarket. These are places to see and be seen, to the extent that Turkish paparazzi hang around waiting for a C-list celebrity to slip on the shiny floors. Many of the malls are out of the centre of town, requiring a taxi or metro ride.

Istiklal Caddesi

Stretching from Tünel Square in the south to Taksim Square in the north, this pedestrianised street is

Whatever your carbon footprint, we can reduce it

For over a decade we've been leading the way in carbon offsetting and carbon management.

In that time we've purchased carbon credits from over 200 projects spread across 6 continents. We work with over 300 major commercial clients and thousands of small and medium sized businesses, which rely upon our market-leading quality assurance programme, our experience and absolute commitment to deliver the right solution for each client.

Why not give us a call?

T: London (020) 7833 6000

Beyoğlu's principal thoroughfare. Busy day and night, Istiklal Caddesi is where modern Istanbul comes for baklava or ice-cream – and to shop. An old tram rattles along the length of the street, past some classic shops. Istiklal was once known for its bookshops, and there are still a couple of good ones here. Robinson Crusoe (see p97) has books in English, and for some interesting ephemera and antiquarian stock, stop by Denizler Kitapevi (see p96), which has sold books for more than 130 years. (The Booksellers' Bazaar, over in the Grand Bazaar, see p65, is also essential for bibliophiles.)

Other relics of the Istiklal of old are its confectionary stalls. Ali Muhiddin Hacı Bekir (see p96), in business since 1777, has a technicolour selection of glorious baklava, halva and *akide* (boiled sweets). For more sugar, Saray (Istiklal Caddesi 102, 0212 292 3434)) has toothsome Turkish desserts.

Once smart, Istiklal Caddesi and the area around it had become run-down and sleazy by the late 1980s. Pedestrianisation set it on the road to recovery, and today the process if more or less complete. Top Shop, Adidas and the Body Shop have predictably moved in, but it still remains the place to pick up clothing bargains, thanks to the covered arcades that sprout off the main road. These fashion *pasajs* are bursting with cheap clothing stacked in bins or hung on rails, all at knock-down prices. A bit of patience, and sharp elbows, help. Many of the clothes are seconds from Turkey's many factories, so you've a good chance of finding recognisable brands.

Antiques & collectibles

Descending downhill east from Istiklal Caddesi is the city's most

---

S H O R T L I S T

Fine foods
- Antre Gourmet Shop (see p114)
- Güllüoğlu (see p116)
- Savoy Pastanesi (see p115)

Best malls
- Kanyon (see p124)
- Istinye Park (see p17)

Best for bookworms
- Booksellers' Bazaar, Grand Bazaar (see p96)
- Denizler Kitapevi (see p96)
- Homer Kitapevi (see p97)
- Robinson Crusoe (see p97)

Elegant fashions
- Berrin Akyüz (see p114)
- Gönül Paksoy (see p20)
- Simay Bülbül (see p89)

Ottoman antiques
- Artrium (see p86)
- Eski Fener (see p111)

Best for rugs
- Ahmet Hazım (see p66)
- Ethnicon (see p67)
- Yörük (see p69)

Quirky souvenirs
- Cocoon (see p63)
- Porof Zihni Sinir (see p111)
- The Works: Objects of Desire (see p111)

Best retro clothing
- Mozk (see p111)
- Roll (see p97)

For all that glitters
- Mor (see p97)
- Sanatanik (see p111)

Best for oenophiles
- Mimolett (see p103)
- Sensus (see p89)

---

idiosyncratic and interesting shopping area: Çukurcuma. The steep winding streets (it's easy to get lost here) are where you'll find most of Istanbul's antique shops. There's also a thriving sector devoted to kitsch and retro items and mid-century modern furniture. You'll find clothing here too: this is where you'll find those vintage sunglasses or an unworn Louis Vuitton dress from the 1940s.

Eski Fener (see p111) is a classic example of a Çukurcuma antique shop; it specialises in furniture, lamps and copperware, mostly sourced from rural Anatolia. But the quirkiest shop in the area is undoubtedly The Works: Objects of Desire (see p111). Focusing on kitsch, mid-century and anything that makes owner Karaca Borar laugh, the shop is a cornucopia of military paraphernalia, old jukeboxes, bumper cars and vintage porn. Hours can happily be spent browsing here. For vintage clothes, Leyla Seyhanlı (see p111) has antique garments, hats and wall hangings, all in excellent condition. Similarly, Mozk (see p111), owned by fashion designers, has vintage leatherwear, dresses and sunglasses.

More unique shops are also appearing in Çukurcuma, thanks to its bohemian vibe and low rents. One example is Porof Zihni Sinir (see p111). Although its pieces are aimed at children, it's full of remarkable inventions that wouldn't be out of place in a Wallace and Gromit animation. Irfan, a cartoonist, also sells books among his fantastical creations.

Following fashion

Fashion designers are also beginning to see Çukurcuma – as well as the already trendy Cihangir – as a suitable locations

Cocoon p63

of boutiques. Simay Bülbül (see p89) sells the young designer's delicate leather and fabric garments. The touches of hide in the dresses and blouses are intricate and feminine. Berrin Akyüz, in Cihangir (see p114) is owned by a designer who splits her time between an atelier and this shop, selling tops, scarves and jewellery. She presents four collections a year with Polish designer Lucasz Budzisz.

But despite incursions into other districts, the upmarket areas of Teşvikiye and Nişantaşı are still design central. These two districts, about a mile north of Taksim Square, are serious label territory. On Abdi İpekçi Caddesi, the likes of Armani, Louis Vuitton and Tiffany sit alongside sophisticated Turkish jewellers. Independent designers with a presence here include Gönül Paksoy (Atiye Sokak 1/3, Teşvikiye, 0212 261 9081), who reinterprets Ottoman designs and traditional weaves and colours.

One of the city's newest shopping areas is in Beşiktaş. Akaretler is a series of redeveloped buildings that were once homes for officers who worked at the nearby Dolmabahçe Palace, the

19th-century residence of the Ottoman sultans. It now houses clothing stores such as Marc Jacobs and Alberta Ferretti and a W hotel.

Craft work

Cheesy souvenirs can be found across the city. Few are the visitors who don't leave Istanbul without an armful of Turkish Delight. Thankfully, tourists wandering around wearing a fez are fairly rare, although they make good souvenirs. Topkapı Palace snow globes apart, then, Turkish handicrafts can be perfect mementos. Ceramics have been made in this area since the 11th century. The predominantly blue and white pottery and tiles from Iznik in western Anatolia was favoured by the sultans and can be found across Istanbul, albeit with dramatic differences in quality. The Istanbul Handicrafts Centre (see p63) in Sultanahmet has goods made by workers on site.

For something completely different, :O (see box p63) has a fun selection of felt hats, hammam wear and four floors of knick-knacks. A couple of doors down is Cocoon's shop for traditional antique clothes and textiles from across Central Asia. It is also a reliable vendor of rugs.

The rug trade

Buying a carpet in Istanbul has unfortunate associations with hassle, hustle and hoodwinking. However, with a bit of homework and common sense, you can enjoy the buying process and go home with a beautiful carpet at the right price. To be a confident and successful bargainer and buyer, you need first to determine how much you are prepared to spend.

Under no circumstances should you tell the dealer your budget. Instead, ask the prices, get a feel for what's on offer, and be prepared to shop around. Look at carpets that are double your price range, and then offer what you have.

If you're interested in hand-made carpets or kilims made of natural fibres, expect to spend YTL450 and above. Many of the rug shops are in the Grand Bazaar, and the ones we have had success with are Ahmet Hazım (see p66) and Ethicon (see p67), which has fixed prices. Other well-regarded carpet shops include Kalender Carpets (see p67) and Yörük (see p69).

Food & drink

After all that bargaining, a drink will be in order. Turkish wines are increasingly recognised as serious drinks by the international wine community. Its signature grape, Öküzgözü, may not be easy to pronounce, but it is easy to knock back. To get a taste of varieties including BoGazkere and Kalecik Karası, Sensus (see p89) offers flights of wines, with a vast selection. Top-class restaurant Mimolett is also a wine boutique (see p103), with more than 400 bottles available. La Cave (see p114) also has a good international selection.

In Cihangir, Antre Gourmet Shop (see p114) has some wines, but it's best known for its Turkish cheeses, yoghurts and olive oils. The Macedonian-owned Sütte (see p102) is another superb deli, with ready-made meze dishes and good meat products.

In Istanbul, some of the best local food products can be found on the streets, especially along Balık Pazarı, off Istiklal Caddesi and Halk Pazarı, opposite the jetty in Beşiktaş.

Reina p131

Nightlife

Forget your preconceptions, Istanbul has a huge propensity to party. On every day of the week, the bars around Beyoğlu fill up after work. After a slight go-home-and-change lull, restaurants get busy and tables in bars get scarce. And after midnight, the clubs turn up the music.

Whether it's live music, designer cocktail lounges, earthy watering holes or pumping clubs, nearly all the city's nightlife options are in Beyoğlu. The really trendy bars and clubs, however, are further along the shores of the Bosphorus in villages such as Ortaköy and Bebek. During summer, many city clubs also decamp up there. This is the place to go if you like your nightlife flashy, and is home to super clubs Reina (see p131) in Ortaköy and Sortie (Muallim Naci Sokak 141-142, 0212 327 8585), on a manmade island off Kuruçeşme.

Many venues try to be all things to all partygoers, with mixed success. It's common to find dinner served until 11pm or so, before the tables are moved away and the DJ hits the decks. Bars will turn the music up as the sun sets, and live music venues will turn the stage over to DJs when bands are scarce.

The party doesn't really get started until after midnight, with clubs peaking between 1am and 4am. Fridays and Saturdays are the busiest nights. There are sometimes special events on Wednesdays. Bars are busy on Thursdays, but it's usually dead in clubs.

To find current information on live music events and club nights, visit the venues or pick up flyers in the cafés and bookshops around Istiklal Caddesi in Beyoğlu. The monthly *Time Out Istanbul* (www.timeoutistanbul.com) in English has listings and previews. For online listings and tickets try: www.pozitif-ist.com, www.echoesproduction.com, www.biletix.com and www.ticketturk.com.

Clubs

Club promoters tend to stick to tried and tested formulas. So although smaller clubs cater to most musical tastes, from rock and jazz to Latin or electronica, the majority of big clubs play house and techno. This is offset by the frequency and variety of guest DJs like Tiesto, Kruder & Dorfmeister, John Digweed and Paul Oakenfold, who take to the turntables here. Istanbul also has plenty of its own talented local DJs: look out for Yunus Güvenen and Murat UncuoGlu.

Istanbul's lively party scene has its idiosyncrasies. Turks definitely like to dress up, so make an effort not to look too casual. You won't find any rowdy, alcohol-induced behaviour at clubs or on the streets. Drinks are generally expensive, due to heavy taxes on alcohol.

New venues crop up every month. One recent addition that looks set to stay is 11:11 (see p92), an ultra-stylish bar with lounges and club floors. A perennial favourite is 360 (see p95), which serves food and cocktails until around midnight, at which point it transforms into a club. Its major asset is the view over the Bosphorus, spectacular as the sun sets. Also with great views, and equally glitzy, is restaurant and club Nu Club (see p92).

Out in Ortaköy, a taxi ride from Taksim, the scene is dominated by the luscious Anjelique (see p128),

DON'T MISS

S H O R T L I S T

Best for glitz
- 11:11 (see p92)
- 360 (see p95)
- Reina (see p131)

Best for live music
- Babylon (see p88)
- Badehane (see p79)
- Peyote (see p102)

For drinks with a view
- 5.Kat (see p112)
- Leb-i Derya Richmond (see p96)
- Nu Teras (see p91)

Hubbly Bubbly bars
- Enjoyer Café (see p61)
- Erenler Çay Bahçesi (see p70)
- Meşale (see p62)

For literary connections
- Büyük Londra Hotel (see p90)
- Pera Palas (see p142)
- Pierre Loti (see p121)

For retro design
- KV Café (see p85)
- Meyra (see p112)
- Simdi (see p86)
- Smyrna (see p114)

Best jazz clubs
- Jazz Café (see p105)
- Nardis (see p90)

Best for big-name DJs
- Anjelique (see p128)
- Public (see p91)

Best wine bars
- Mimolett (see p103)
- Pano (see p101)
- Sensus (see p89)

Best gay bars
- Bigudi Pub (see p102)
- Tek Yön (see p94)

the upmarket Blackk (Muallim Naci Caddesi 71, Ortaköy, 0212 236 7256, www.blackk.net) and the superclub Reina (see p131). These are places to enjoy chilled (pricey) cocktails, with killer Bosphorus views.

If bling isn't your thing, there's no shortage of more alternative and underground clubbing. Venues such as Dirty (see p97), known for its pop-art decor and interesting DJs, Dogzstar (see p97), a small venue that's popular among a more punky fraternity, and live music and alternative club Peyote (see p102) in the heart of Nevizade Sokak, can all make for great nights out.

Music

Music of some kind can be heard everywhere you go. Buskers are popular along Istiklal Caddesi, and from the bars, a mixture of pop, rock and arabesque blasts out. Live music, formerly a little lacklustre, is now easily accessible. Whether it's the latest punk band, gypsy musicians or traditional *fasıl* music, all is widely accessible.

Most of Istanbul's music venues are located on the side-streets off Istiklal Caddesi, making it easy to keep up with what's going on – though it helps if you're prepared to tolerate cramped and smoky conditions. One of the key venues is Babylon (see p88). With an exciting and innovative roster of events, this is perhaps the city's best music venue for rock, world jazz and pop. The management also runs the Doublemoon record label (www.doublemoon.com.tr). Other superb venues for live bands include Balans (see p102), which has occasional international big hitters and Turkish stars, and Peyote (see p102), which is more alternative. Indigo (see p99) is a nightclub, but it also hosts cutting-edge electronic acts.

For traditional *fasıl* music, simply head to the restaurants on Nevizade to hear the wandering musicians – it's common for groups to interrupt their meal and start dancing. Even people strolling along Istiklal might find time to stop for a dance in front of buskers.

For dedicated folk music venues, try Eylül (see p99) or the highly recommended Munzur (see p105). To see one of Turkey's finest musicians, the gypsy jazz clarinettist Selim Sesler, try Badehane (see p79) on Wednesday night, where the great man often plays. The venue has live music throughout the week; check the board in the bar for details.

In Istanbul, jazz has a revered status, with a hard core of devotees and musicians who keep the scene varied and vibrant. Jazz is the focus of the prestigious International Jazz Festival (see p33), the Akbank Jazz Festival (see p36) and a wonderful jazz bar called Nardis (see p90). Both

360 p95

International Jazz Festival p33

festivals draw a glittering array of global stars (partly because they use a very broad definition of jazz); thanks to Nardis, the line-ups feature strong local players, too. The Jazz Café (see p105) is another good venue, with regular sessions from guitarist Bülent Ortaçgil.

Gay & lesbian

While Turkey's strictly secular nature means the gay community is not subjected to the ranting of religious figures, the traditional family structure is still firmly in place, and there is enormous pressure to marry. A high premium is placed on knuckle-dragging masculinity, which is one reason why so many bisexual and gay men present themselves in public as straight. Nevertheless, Istanbul still a vibrant gay nightlife scene.

There are bars and clubs, Turkish baths are as steamy as ever, cyber hook-ups are an increasingly favoured sexual and social outlet for the closeted majority, and secluded public parks are wildly cruisey. But if you come to Istanbul expecting

to find a gay nightlife scene comparable to that of major cities in the US and Europe, you will be disappointed – although incredible strides have been made.

The venues can be divided in to two types: Western clubs, where the scene is similar to Europe or the US, and Turkish-style (a la Turca) which have more complicated social dynamics.

Needless to say, most of the bars, clubs and cafés are in Beyoğlu, with Balo Sokak, off Istiklal Caddesi, the central thread. The long-standing Sugar Café (Sakasalim Çıkmazı, off Istiklal Caddesi, 0212 244 1276) is a good starting point to meet people. Other good bars in the area include the lesbian Bigudi Pub (see p102) and Other Side (see p106). There are few bona fide clubs, all of which draw a mixed, rather than exclusively gay, crowd. Among them ar Xlarge (see p94) and Privé (see p106).

To venture into the a la Turca scene, try clubs Déjà Vu (Sadri Alışık Sokak 26/1, 0535 614 8164)) or TekYön (see p94), or the Chianti Café-Pub (Balo Sokak 31/2).

Santralistanbul p119

WHAT'S BEST

Arts & Leisure

In 2010, Istanbul was a European Capital of Culture. With more events, festivals and exhibitions than ever before, it was seen by many as a turning point on the Istanbul cultural scene.

Istanbullus have known all along that their city had a vibrant arts community, a slow-burning but resurgent film industry (with a couple of Oscar nominations, including Mahsun Kırmızıgül's *Güneşi Gördüm, I Saw the Sun*), and a theatre industry that is thriving thanks to new venues such as Garajistanbul (see p99).

The city also knows how to put on a festival, with world-class events throughout the year. The most significant, held every two years (the next is in 2011), is the International Istanbul Biennial, at the ever-improving Istanbul

Modern (see p115). The annual film festival and theatre festival are also growing in stature. Smaller festivals such as the International Puppet Festival (see box p34) and the Akbank Jazz Festival (see p36) offer increasingly diverse and popular performances.

Tickets for concerts, opera and theatre, and sports events, can be bought online from Biletex (www.biletix.com).

Art

Several recently opened venues reflect a burgeoning art scene. Back in 2004, Istanbul Modern opened in an old customs warehouse on the Bosphorus. Alongside a fairly standard collection of Turkish art, dating from the 20th century to the present, the museum showcases interesting recent acquisitions and stages several temporary exhibitions each year.

Hot on the heels of Istanbul Modern came the Pera Museum (see p90), with a historical collection displayed alongside work by young contemporary artists. Meanwhile, the Sakip Sabanci Museum (see p128) raised its profile with exhibitions of works by the likes of Picasso and Rodin.

The most recent arrival is the vast Santralistanbul arts and cultural complex (see p119), opened in 2007 in a converted power station. It has become an essential venue for multimedia exhibitions, as well as concerts and workshops.

Most of Istanbul's best art galleries are funded by the private sector, banks in particular. Most of these galleries have high-profile locations along Istiklal Caddesi. Among them, Galerist (Mısır Apartment 311/4, 0212 244 8230, www.galerist.com.tr) and Casa Dell'Arte (Mısır Apartment 163/3, 0212 251 4288, www.casadellarte gallery.com) have outstanding exhibition programmes featuring both Turkish and foreign artists. The latest addition to the bunch is the multidisciplinary Arter (see box p95), with five floors of videos, paintings, photography and installations. Meanwhile, several hotels, among them Çırağan Palace Kempinski (see p148) and Tomtom Suites (see p145), have started to host exhibitions.

Theatre

Theatre in Istanbul is far more vital and varied than the classical music, opera or ballet scenes. More than 30 stages are scattered across the city, some in the remotest districts. For a healthy mix

SHORTLIST

Best performing arts festivals
- Istanbul Theatre Festival (see p32)
- International Puppet Festival (see p32)

Most interesting shows
- Garajistanbul (see p99)
- International Istanbul Theatre Festival (see p32)
- Muhsin ErtuGrul Stage (see p29)

Best classical concert halls
- Atatürk Cultural Centre (see p106)
- Cemal Reşit Rey Concert Hall (see p30)
- Enka Ibrahim Betil Auditorium (see p30)

Best film festivals
- IF AFM Independent Film Festival (see p31)
- International Istanbul Film Festival (see p32)

Best for modern art
- Arter (see p95)
- Casa Dell'Arte (see left)
- Santralistanbul (see p119)

For blockbuster exhibitions
- Istanbul Modern (see p115)
- Pera Museum (see p90)
- Sakip Sabanci Museum (see p128)

Best music festivals
- International Istanbul Jazz Festival (see p33)
- Rock 'n' Coke (see p35)

Best for new Turkish Art
- Casa Dell'Arte (see left)
- Galerist (see left)
- Santralistanbul (see p119)

Offset your
flight with
Trees for Cities
and make your
trip mean
something for
years to come

www.treesforcities.org/offset

Trees for Cities
Charity registration number 1032154

Muhsin Ertuğrul Stage

of classic and contemporary productions (in Turkish), check out the City Players (Kent Oyuncuları), starring Yıldız Kenter, at the Kenter Theatre (Halaskargazi Caddesi 9/B, Harbiye, 0212 246 3589, www.kentersinema tiyatro.com). Garajistanbul (see p99), in Beyoğlu, offers some of the most cutting-edge productions in the city, whether it's theatre, world music, new opera or children's pieces. The stalwart Muhsin Ertuğrul Stage (3 Gümüş Caddesi, Harbiye, 0212 455 3919, www.ibst.gov.tr).) was founded in 1914 and stages classical productions with low ticket prices. And the Atatürk Cultural Centre (see p106) will stage plays once again when it reopens, which is scheduled for the end of 2010. Be aware that many theatres are closed from June to September.

The best chance for seeing good theatre in English is the International Istanbul Theatre Festival (see p32), organised by the Istanbul Foundation for Culture and Arts (www.iksv.org/ english), and the Location Theatre Festival (Mekan Tiyatro Festivali), organised by the Istanbul Metropolitan Municipality. Both feature performances from dozens of foreign companies, with performances staged in their original languages.

Classical music

Turkey doesn't have a long tradition of Western classical music. The Ottomans had their own courtly music, but Atatürk, who considered it regressive and elitist, banned it. Today, however, Istanbul is home to a respectable – if small – classical music, opera and ballet scene. Although the choice is pretty limited, Istanbul has some decent symphonic and chamber music orchestras, and also hosts the major annual International Istanbul Music Festival (see p33).

The city's modern venues are also very good, if few; chief among them is the Atatürk Cultural Centre (closed until the end of 2010), where the Istanbul Symphony Orchestra and the Istanbul State Opera and Ballet company perform, along with foreign companies.

Other venues worth checking out include Akbank Culture and Arts Centre (see p106), Bosphorus University Albert Long Hall Cultural Centre (Bebek, 0212 359 5400), Enka Ibrahim Betil Auditorium (Sadi Gülçelik Spor Sitesi, Istinye, 0212 276 2214, www.enkasanat.org) and the Cemal Reşit Rey Concert Hall (Darülbedai Caddesi 1, Harbiye, 0212 232 9830, www.crrks.org).

Film

Istanbul's movie-goers are well served, with more than 200 screens, an annual world-class film festival and several smaller cinematic events. The dominance of Hollywood blockbusters still prevails, but a handful of cinemas now specialise in independent and art-house films, including those of Turkish provenance. Big names in the Turkish film world include Cannes winner Nuri Bilge Ceylan, creator of the acclaimed *Uzak* (*Distant*) and the brutally realist Zeki Demirkubuz, who also wowed the Cannes crowd with *Kader* (*Destiny*). Young directors are also being increasingly recognised, notably Yüksel Aksu, for his *Ice Scream, I Scream.*

The best cinemas are in Beyoğlu. The Emek (see p99) is a grand old picture house dating from the 1920s. The best art-house picture house is Yeşilçam (Imam Adnan Sokak 10, off Istiklal Caddesi, 0212 293 6800, www.yesilcam sinemasi.com), which has a good programme of local and European independent film. Istanbul Modern (see p115) has a state-of-the-art cinema, which runs a monthly programme dedicated to home-grown and international

art-house movies, including retrospectives, documentaries, animation and shorts.

Istanbul hosts a film event almost every week of the year. Needless to say, some are more worthwhile than others. The main cinematic event of the year is the International Istanbul Film Festival (see p31), a highlight of the Turkish cultural calendar, held each spring.

Sport

Istanbul loves football. Galatasary, Beşiktaş and Fenerbahçe have all, at one time or another, inspired fear in their European opponents (and visiting fans). The Black Sea side Trabzonspor supposedly completes the 'big four,' but has struggled to keep up in recent years. The domestic league runs from August to May and has a lopsided feel, as little clubs line up for a battering from the Istanbul heavyweights. For a really intense atmosphere, try to catch one of the Istanbul derbies. Games can feel a little intimidating if you go alone; much better to go along with a local if you can. The noise is terrific.

Basketball is also very popular in Istanbul, and even has its own NBA superstar, Mehmet Okur, who plays with Utah Jazz. Turkey's basketball season lasts from October to June, with clubs playing at least twice a week, usually in the afternoon or early evening. Information on games and fixtures is available on the Turkish Basketball Federation website (www.tbf.org.tr). The main teams are Beşiktaş ColaTurka, Efes Pilsen and Fenerbahçe-Ülker.

All sporting events and fixtures are listed in the local press and at the online ticketing agency Biletix (www.biletix.com) or Ticket Turk (www.ticketturk.com).

Calendar

International Istanbul Jazz Festival p33

When the republic was founded in 1923, Ottoman imperial traditions and overt religious celebrations were replaced by a dour bunch of annual excuses for flag-waving, such as Republic Day (29 October) and Victory Day (30 August). In recent years, though, the full-blown festive spirit has returned to the city. Nowadays, winter apart, every month sees a festival some kind. Many of these events are superbly managed by the Istanbul Foundation for Arts and Cultures (Istanbul Kültür ve Sanat Vakfı; www.iksv.org), which consistently attracts a roster of international big names.

Dates highlighted in **bold** indicate public holidays.

January

1 Jan **New Year's Day**

February

Feb **IF AFM Independent Film Festival**
AFM Fitaş (www.ifistanbul.com)
This hugely popular event is run by the cinema chain AFM. The programming is distinctly right-on, with strands dedicated to digital, political, and gay/lesbian cinema, plus hardcore sex and violence.

April

April **International Istanbul Film Festival**
Various venues
www.iksv.org
An annual highlight, eagerly anticipated for the glamour factor of visiting movie stars. Be warned, though: this is the city's most popular cultural jamboree, and tickets sell out well in advance.

**International Istanbul
Film Festival p31**

Apr/May **Orthodox Easter**
Patrikhane (Orthodox Patriarchate
Building)
0212 531 9674
The city's last remaining Greek residents – as well as hundreds of pilgrims from Greece – flock to Easter Sunday mass in the venerable Patriarchate in Fener. In a church illuminated by hundreds of candles, the aura of ancient ritual is powerful enough to move even the most ardent of atheists.

**23 April National Sovereignty
& Children's Day**

May

May (even years) **International
Istanbul Theatre Festival**
Various venues
0212 334 0700/334 0777,
www.iksv.org
One of the few opportunities to see international theatre in Istanbul. In the past, big draws have included the likes of Robert Wilson, Pina Bausch, the Berliner Ensemble, the Piccolo

Teatro di Milano and Britain's Royal Shakespeare Company. The programme also features a selection of the year's best Turkish plays. Most performances are held at city theatres but a few events take place at more unusual venues, such as Rumeli Hisarı on the Bosphorus.

2nd week of May **International
Istanbul Puppet Festival**
Kenter Theatre and other venues
www.kuklaistanbul.org/en
Puppet, marionette and shadow theatre was big in Ottoman times, but is rarely performed today. This festival is an opportunity to witness this almost forgotten art, with around a dozen shows by Turkish and international companies. Most plays are silent and suitable for children and adults.

19 May Youth & Sports Day

late May **Conquest Week
Celebrations**
Various venues
www.ibb.gov.tr

A lively celebration of the Turkish conquest of Constantinople (29 May 1453), featuring exhibitions of traditional Turkish arts and parades by the 'Ottoman' Mehter band, plus concerts, conferences, lectures, screenings, fireworks and some rabble-rousing by nationalist and Islamist parties.

June

June-July **International Istanbul Music Festival**
Various venues
www.iksv.org
Inaugurated in 1973 on the occasion of the 50th anniversary of the republic, the IMF is the most prestigious event on the city's cultural calendar. It comprises about 30 performances of orchestra and chamber music, dance and ballet. Big hitters at past festivals have included Kiri Te Kanawa, Philip Glass, the Michael Nyman Ensemble, Cecilia Bartoli and the Kronos Quartet.

July

Ongoing International Istanbul Music Festival (see June)

July **International Istanbul Jazz Festival**
Various venues
www.iksv.org
This two-week festival pushes the boundaries of what defines modern jazz. Keith Jarrett, Wynton Marsalis and Dizzy Gillespie have all performed in the 4,000-seat Harbiye open-air theatre, as have less likely musicians like Grace Jones, Nick Cave, Lou Reed and Martha Wainwright. Consistently the best programme of any Turkish music festival.

mid July-early Aug **Traditional Istanbul Açıkhava (Open-Air) Concerts**
Harbiye Cemil Topuzlu, Açıkhava Tiyatrosu
www.mostproduction.com

Bosphorus breaststroke

The Bosphorus Cross-Continental is the world's only intercontinental swimming race. It begins at the Kanlıca pier on the Asian shore and finishes at a pier in Kuruçeşme, on the European shore, a distance of 6.5 kilometres (four miles). Depths can be up to 100 metres.

Run by the Turkish Olympic Committee, the race started in 1989 with 70 swimmers. Today, the limited number of places for this popular annual event, held each July, are snapped up quickly.

From the shoreline, the Bosphorus looks blue, calm and tranquil. But head out in a small boat, and the swells can be unexpectedly high. This is a busy, working stretch of water. The narrow strait may be scenic but – with giant tankers, speedboats, fishing vessels and passenger ferries passing at close quarters – it can also be hazardous. However, a section of the waterway is closed off for the duration of the race, to allow the several hundred brave competitors to dive into the choppy waters, and emerge on shore on a different continent.

The average time for swimmers to make the crossing is 50 minutes, but times vary with conditions – they may not have to deal with passing vessels, but it's easy to lose sight of fellow competitors behind a wave in this race.
■ www.bosphorus.cc

Puppet state

In Ottoman times, shadow puppet plays were a common form of entertainment, with troupes of puppeteers setting up makeshift stage in public squares, particularly during Ramadan.

Thought to be influenced by travelling theatre from Asia, it is believed that puppetry became popular in the area that is now Turkey around the 12th century.

In 2010, UNESCO awarded Karagöz – Turkish shadow theatre, which uses leather puppets – the status of an 'intangible cultural element'. Like Punch and Judy, Karagöz comes with a cast of characters. The principals are Karagöz himself, an illiterate, straightforward commoner, and Hacivat, an educated and verbose Ottoman. Tradition has it that the characters are based on workers building a mosque in Bursa during the rule of Orhan 1 (1326-1359).

The satire, in which Karagöz often gets the better of Hacivat thanks to his streetwise thinking, was popular among all social strata during the Ottoman era, and the tradition has been maintained into the present. Plays rely on the wit and skill of the puppet master,

as puppeteer, mimic (he voices every character) and writer.

With this rich heritage, it's apt that Istanbul that holds an annual International Puppet Festival (see p32), a highlight of the cultural year. Founded by famed puppet scholar Cengiz Özek in 1998, the 2010 event featured 75 performances by 25 groups from 15 countries. The programme included free, nightly performances of Vietnamese water puppet theatre in Taksim Square and dozens of plays with the 2010 festival's Shakespeare theme. Some shows pushed the boundaries of traditional puppetry and included innovative multimedia work. One featured live dancers interacting with puppets and video to a musical soundtrack.

The festival's main venue is the Kukla Istanbul (Taksim Akarcası Sokak 4, Tehit Muhtar Mahallesi), Istanbul's dedicated puppet theatre. Cengiz Özek's own puppet collection is on display here during the festival. Other performances are held at the French Cultural Centre, the Istanbul Metropolitan Municipality City Theatre and Garajistanbul (see p99).

This season of open-air concerts in Harbiye is worth checking out. The line-up mixes mainstream names from Turkish pop, rock and folk with a variety of alternative genres. It's a good opportunity to see the more innovative end of the local music scene. Past performers have included the Mercan Dede Fusion Project, alongside Balkan stars such as Goran Bregovic.

August

Ongoing Traditional Istanbul Açıkhava (Open-Air) Concerts (see July)

1-30 Aug 2011 **Ramazan**
Muslims abstain from food, drink, smoking and sex between dawn and dusk. Ramazan nights are the busiest of the year in religious districts such as Fatih. The end of Ramazan is marked by the three-day Şeker Bayramı or 'Sugar Holiday', when sweets are traditionally given to friends and family.

30 Aug **Victory Day**

September

early Sept, odd years
Rock 'n' Coke
Hezarfen Airfield
www.pozitif-ist.com,
www.rockncoke.com
Since it began in 2003, Rock 'n' Coke has become Istanbul's biggest (late) summer opportunity to stand in a beer queue with 50,000 of your closest friends. Groups appearing at past events have included the Prodigy, Nine Inch Nails, Linkin Park, the Smashing Pumpkins and Franz Ferdinand. Turkey's largest open-air festival is now held every two years; the next will be in 2011.

Sept-Nov, odd years **International Istanbul Biennial**
Various venues
www.iksv.org
Alternating with the Istanbul Theatre Festival, every other year more than 50 artists from around 50 countries exhibit around a theme set by a guest curator. Expect to find paintings, installations, screenings, walkabouts, films,

International Istanbul Biennial

panel discussions, lectures and guided tours (in English). The next Biennial will be held in 2011 and will be curated by Adriano Pedrosa and Jens Hoffmann.

Oct

Ongoing International Istanbul Biennial (see Sept)

Oct **Akbank Jazz Festival**
Various venues
www.pozitif-ist.com
Unlike July's international jamboree (see p33), this festival is less about big names and more about jazz. Some ten bands perform every day over a two-week period, with jam sessions at venues including Babylon (see p88) and Nardis (see p90). Joe Lavano, Marilyn Mazur and Cecil Taylor have all participated in recent years. In addition to great music, there are film screenings and workshops.

29 Oct **Republic Day**

late Oct-early Nov **Phonem/ Electronic Music Plateau**
Various venues
www.iksv.org
An international platform for exploring electronic music, with discussions, technology exhibitions and performances. Expect a string of parties featuring local and international DJs, plus concerts, video art, film and video screenings, and workshops.

Oct-Nov **Istanbul Arts Fair**
Tüyap Centre, E5 Hwy (Karayolu), Gürpınar Jcn, Kavşağı, Beylikdüzü
www.tuyap.com.tr
Relocated from its city centre home to the less accessible Tüyap Centre near the airport, this vast, week-long sales fair has retained its massive appeal. Some 50 Istanbul galleries plus a handful of international art dealers come to offload paintings, sculpture and ceramics. Don't let the remote location put you off: free shuttle services depart from AKM on Taksim Square, Atatürk airport, the Bakırköy ferry stop and the Esenler bus terminal.

November

Ongoing International Istanbul Biennial (see Sept); Phonem Electronic Music Plateau (see Oct); Istanbul Arts Fair (see Oct).

10 Nov **Anniversary of Atatürk's Death**
Every 10 November at 9.05am, the death of Mustafa Kemal Atatürk is marked with a minute's silence. Sirens howl mournfully and the Bosphorus ferries sound their foghorns, while buses, cars, and people everywhere come to a sudden standstill. The experience is both moving and eerie – a testament to the great leader's lasting grip on the Turkish public's imagination.

17 Nov 2010, 6 Nov 2011 **Feast of the Sacrifice (Kurban Bayramı)**

Nov **Istanbul Book Fair**
Tüyap Centre, E5 Hwy (Karayolu), Gürpınar Jcn Kavşağı, Beylikdüzü
www.tuyap.com.tr
Over 200 Turkish publishing houses, plus publishers from abroad, gather for ten days to trade their wares. Leading writers, academics and intellectuals participate in conferences and roundtable discussions. Free shuttle services run from AKM on Taksim Square, Atatürk airport, the Bakırköy ferry stop and Esenler bus terminal.

Nov-Dec **Efes Pilsen Blues Festival**
Lütfü Kırdar Convention Centre, Harbiye
www.pozitif-ist.com
This hugely popular festival, running since 1990, is a showcase for new talent, with three bands performing every night. This doesn't stop the occasional star (such as Bobby Rush or Long John Hunter) from showing up.

Itineraries

Haghia Sophia p54

Istanbul Through the Ages

Byzantium, Nova Roma, Constantinople and Istanbul: whatever the city on the Bosphorus has been called, it has – from the fourth century until the advent of the republic – been at the heart of an empire. And through the years, various rulers have endeavoured to mark their place in history on Istanbul's eclectic skyline.

Our itinerary follows Istanbul's development through the ages, taking in the defining monuments erected by successive leaders over two millennia. We start with the clatter of racing chariots at the beginning of the Roman occupation and finish more than 2,000 years later with the troubled birth of Turkey, and the symbolic heart of the republic, Taksim Squre. Many of the attractions along the route can take up to a day to explore in themselves, but this itinerary is designed to give an overview of the

history of Istanbul in a day, with refreshment stops along the way.

For an in-depth view of the history of Istanbul from its conception, visit the comprehensive **Archaeology Museum** (p53), which is particularly strong on the Roman era.

There is nothing left standing of the original Greek settlement of Byzantium, which was founded in 658 BC. Others were quick to recognise the strategic importance of the new city, and it was repeatedly taken by warring regional powers. In AD 73, it was incorporated into the Roman province of Bithynia. By the end of the third century, the Roman Empire had become too unwieldy to govern effectively from Rome, and it was subdivided, with part of the power shifted to Byzantium. In 324, Constantine, Emperor of the West, defeated Licinius, Emperor of the East. On 11 May 330, Constantine inaugurated his new seat of power

Topkapı Palace p49

as 'Nova Roma', a name by which the city has never been known since – its people, and historians, preferring Constantinople.

Our journey begins at the only remaining monument of Constantine's reign: the **Serpentine Column** (see p54) – carried off from the Temple of Apollo at Delphi, where it had been set to commemorate Greek victory over the Persians in 480 BC. It is now located on the **Hippodrome** (see p54), an arena used for racing, ceremonies and coronations. Opposite the Serpentine Column is the **Egyptian obelisk** (see p54), originally carved in 1500 BC and moved to Constantinople in 390 AD by emperor Theodosius.

Justinian, the most architecturally prolific Byzantine emperor, provided the city with immense water cisterns including our next stop, **Yerebatan Sarnıc** (see p59) across Divan Yolu. The atmospheric underground space still draws appreciative gasps from visitors.

He also bequeathed more than 40 churches. Justinian's finest moment is also Istanbul's: **Haghia Sophia** (see p54). You can't miss its rather ugly façade, but the interior, with its stunning dome, is remarkable if rather bare today. For close to a thousand years this was the greatest church in Eastern Christendom. Dedicated on 26 December AD 537, the dome was the largest ever built; it is said it was made of such thin material that the hundreds of candles hung high within would cause it to glow at night like a golden beacon.

Haghia Sophia's destiny over the next millennium reflected the city's. Emperor Leo III was an iconoclast, believing that venerating icons was equivalent to the worship of graven images. There was widespread vandalism of icons and images during this period, including mosaics in Haghia Sophia. Once this dark era had passed, the first new mosaic was unveiled in 867 – a Madonna and child – which can still be seen today. Western crusaders, too, did more than their fare share of damage, ransacking the cathedral in 1204, and carrying off everything they could.

The most important date in the city's history is 28 May 1453, when the Ottomans finally breached the city walls (for more on these events, take a detour to the Panorama 1453 History Museum, see p122). Mehmet II turned Haghia Sophia into a mosque, building four minarets. He also built the centrepiece of the Ottoman Empire, **Topkapı Palace** (see p49).

Walk around the back Haghia Sophia on Sultanahmet Square, along Babıhümayun Caddesi, to the Imperial Gate, stopping off at the lovely **Yeşil Ev Beer Garden** (see p63) if you feel in need of refreshment. You could spend a day wandering around the Topkapı Palace (and given the admission fee, its worth dedicating some time). While Mehmet II made Istanbul the Ottoman capital, it was during the 46-year reign of Süleyman the Magnificent (1520-66) that the city became a true imperial centre, with this palace, gilded by the wealth, tributes and taxes from newly conquered territories, its focus.

From Topkapı Palace, walk downhill towards the Golden Horn, following the tram route (or take the tram if you feel like it). Passing Sirkeci Station (see p71), the final destination of the Orient Express, the frantically busy Bosphorus and mouth of the Golden Horn will come into view. If you are hungry, stop at **Hamdi Et Lokantası** (see p75) for some fine traditional Turkish food.

Head along the docks to Galata Bridge. High on the hill to the west is the **Süleymaniye Mosque** (see p70), an exquisite and dominating construction designed by Süleyman the Magnificent's head architect Mimar Sinan in 1557.

Souvenir shoppers will want to take a detour into the **Egyptian Bazaar** (see p71), named for its links with the Cairo caravan, a flotilla of ships that arrived annually with spices, rice and coffee.

On the other side of Galata Bridge you enter a different world. The districts of Galata and Pera (modern-day Beyoğlu) was originally a non-Muslim, European district. Originally founded as an Italian traders' enclave in Byzantine times, by the 17th century it was a multiethnic city. However, it really came into its own in the 19th century, developing into a commercial and entertainment district centred on the Grande Rue de Pera, location for an increasing number of theatres, cafés, bars and hotels. Istanbul was shifting its locus from south of the Golden Horn to north.

Following the route of the Orient Express travellers, climb up the steep hill – or take the underground funicular, built in 1876. It will deposit you in the heart of Beyoğlu. From here walk up the pedestrianised Istiklal Caddesi, or Independence Avenue, formerly Grande Rue de Pera but renamed after the birth of the republic by Mustafa Kemal, known as Atatürk (father of the Turks). Most of the existing buildings in Beyoğlu date back to the 19th century, although there are some wonderful examples of early 20th-century art nouveau architecture.

Continue up Istiklal Caddesi, avoiding the tram and weaving through the evening crowds, to its conclusion at Taksim Square. It is in not a pretty end to the walk – it's a busy, traffic-clogged transport hub. Nevertheless, it is the symbolic heart of the secular republic, and home to the Independence Monument, in honour of the new republic. Here, make an about-turn, and head to the restaurants and bars off Istiklal Caddesi, in locations such as Nevizade Sokak, Tünel Square or Asmalımescit, to get a good feel for Istanbul life in the 21st century.

Ortaköy p126

The City by Night

Many visitors are a little surprised by Istanbul after dark. Istiklal Caddesi, Beyoğlu's main street, gets busier as the sun sets and bars and restaurants fill up with lively drinkers and diners every night of the week. Evenings on the narrow streets around Tünel and Nevizade Sokak show Istanbul at its most raucous – and it can be very raucous. Yet walk in any direction off the main drag and you'll find a city that is relaxing from its long day in a more reserved manner. Men line the streets shuffling backgammon pieces and drinking endless glasses of tea. Women sit on doorsteps chatting while their children play nearby.

Night-time in Istanbul is interesting wherever you wander. But best of all is when you turn a corner to an unexpected panorama of the glimmering Bosphorus, still busy with commuter ferries, party boats and cruise ships. The reason for the popularity of evening cruises among visitors and boat-top festivities among Istanbullus is obvious – the view from the water of the floodlit domes and minarets of Sultanahmet, the nightly lightshow on the first Bosphorus bridge and the spectacle of Topkapı Palace are little short of magical.

Our tour of Istanbul by night begins with a relaxing boat trip, the best way to get your bearings in the city.

As the evening sun takes on a golden hue, head down to the docks at Eminönü. From this busy wharf, Istanbul's workers will be returning to their homes on the other side of the Bosphorus, a continent away. We join them on a passenger ferry to Üsküdar on the Asian shore – YTL1.50 each way.

As the ferry emerges from the Golden Horn, a grand vista opens out. To the south, dozens of huge cargo ships sway on the Sea of Marmara; to the north, the sun

Badehane p79

sets on the 14th-century **Galata Tower** (see p79), rising above Beyoğlu; to the east is the Asian shore, gateway to Anatolia. Most eyes, however, turn west and to Sultanahmet, the spit to the south of the Golden Horn. Chugging past Topkapı Palace allows you to realise the impressive scale of the fortress, for centuries the hub of the Ottoman Empire. Rising over Sultanahmet is its namesake mosque, also known as the **Blue Mosque** (see p59). Built in the early 1600s, it is distinctive because of its six minarets – a decision that provoked hostility at the time of its construction: six minarets had previously been reserved for the Prophet's mosque. As the sun sets, floodlights spark up to stunning effect. (There are occasional light shows here at 9pm during the summer.)

Further across the Bosphorus, the boat will glide past **Kız Kulesi** (Maiden's Tower). It was supposedly named after a princess who was confined here after a prophet predicted she would die from a snakebite: the fatal bite was duly delivered by a serpent that arrived in a basket of fruit. These days, the tower is a café-restaurant.

Üsküdar, like many settlements along the Asian shore, is quieter than much of the European shore. It's a good place to wander to experience the more traditional face of Istanbul. When you're ready to come back, simply get on the ferry.

Back in Eminönü, head for the **Galata Bridge** (see p72). This bridge is more than a route from one shore to another. This is actually the fifth Galata Bridge that has stood here, but since the first one was constructed in 1845 it has been a gathering place for Istanbullus. This one was built in the 1980s to accommodate growing traffic. It has two decks: below are lively restaurants, bars and teahouses; traffic and pedestrians travel above. The smell of diesel and rattle of trams take some of the romance out of the walk, but only a little. You can still take in the aromas of fish being cooked on makeshift barbecues by the many fishermen who cast their lines here, mingling with sellers of bagel-like *simit* and grilled corn on the cob.

Once over the bridge, turn right along the promenade, catching the cool breeze and salty air of the Bosphorus, and head into

Karaköy and Tophane. These neighbourhoods are untouched by the gentrification consuming much of Beyoğlu. Walk along Rıhtım Caddesi and Kemankeş Caddesi, following the tram route. As night falls, Turkish men (it's always men) gather in cafés to play backgammon or cards, and to chat. During the summer they spill out on to the pavements.

Just off Tophane Iskelesi are dozens of narghile cafés (see box p55) – places where students, locals and in-the-know tourists go to smoke the hookah, hubbly bubbly or waterpipe. The Turks have been smoking the narghile since the 17th century, and despite it being banned at various times over the last 300 years, it has become very popular again: once there was just a small row of cafés here, now there are lots of them. Just sit down and choose from the menu of tobaccos (bear in mind that the fruity ones aren't everybody's cup of tea).

Resist the temptation to spend the night on the cushions and instead walk up Defterdar Yokuťu Sokak to Akarsu Yokuşu Sokak, in the heart of Istanbul's trendiest neighbourhood: Cihangir. Along this little stretch are some of the city's best western-style cafés. On warm nights, the windows of **Meyra** (see p112) open out on to the streets, perfect for people-watching. A little further along is **Smyrna** (see p114) a retro classic and Cihangir favourite. For food, one of the city's best fish restaurants, **Doğa Balık** (see p112), also has wonderful views over the city, as does the opulent bar and restaurant **Beşinci Kat** (see p112) on Soğancı Sokak.

Turn right on to Siraselviler Caddesi and walk towards Taksim Square. Here, the crowd thickens. Hawkers of toys and tat hound passersby, and kebab sellers do a brisk trade. Looking down Istiklal Caddesi from Taksim in the evening is an impressive sight. Hundreds of Istanbullus fill the wide pedestrian street, shopping (stores close around 9pm or 10pm) and socialising.

Now its time to eat. And where else but Nevizade Sokak? This bustling, noisy little street is lined with restaurants and bars, many of them traditional *meyhanes* (taverns). These are the places where locals meet to eat, drink, and perhaps sing along with the house musicians. All the seats are filled by garrulous diners, attended by dashing waiters and hopeful street vendors. **Krependeki Imroz** (see p101), founded in 1941, is one of the oldest *meyhanes* in Istanbul, and one of our favourites, although there is little to choose between them.

There's plenty of nightlife in the area if you want to continue your evening. For clubs, try the upmarket **11:11** (see p92). Nearby **Babylon** (see p88) and **Peyote** (see p102) offer different entertainment, often with rock bands on one floor and alternative music on another. No prizes for guessing the music at the **Nardis Jazz Club** (see p90) and **Jazz Café** (see p105). **Badehane** (see p79) also has gypsy jazz on some nights – local clarinet legend Selim Sesler often plays on Wednesday nights. And if you need a late-night shot of energy, join other party people at Saray (Istiklal Caddesi 102, 0212 292 3434). Its *aşure*, a milk pudding, is renowned, but all of its sweet treats are wonderful.

However, we would recommend ending the night as we began – with sensational scenes over the Bosphorus. There are great views, and thumping music, at **360** (see p95). But for a chilled drink, try **Leb-i Derya Richmond** (see p96) or its new branch nearby, Leb-i Derya Kumbarcı (Kumbarcı Yokuu 57/6, 0212 293 4989).

ITINERARIES

Galata Bridge p72

Literary City

Istanbul is a city that inspires. Memoirists and poets, novelists and journalists have been transfixed by the contradictions, the beauty, the exoticism, the decrepitude, the immigrants, the residents, the sultans and the politicians. In turn, those same writers shape our view of Istanbul. Just as New York looks like a Woody Allen movie, so Istanbul reads like an Orhan Pamuk novel.

In *Istanbul: Memories and the City*, Nobel Prize-winning Turkish novelist Pamuk writes: 'For me [Istanbul] has always been a city of ruins and of end-of-empire melancholy. I've spent my life either battling with this melancholy, or (like all Istanbullus) making it my own.'

So melancholy. So grey. It isn't, of course, and Orhan Pamuk realises this. He is aware that he views Istanbul through a fog of nostalgia and black-and-white photos. And he is not alone. He

has written of the 'four melancholic writers' AS Hisar, Yahya Kemal, Resat Ekrem Koçu and Ahmet Hamdi Tanpınar: 'The Istanbul in which they lived was a city littered with ruins of the great fall, but it was their city. If they gave themselves to melancholic poems about loss and destruction, they would, they discovered, find a voice all of their own.'

Pamuk is acutely aware of the importance of belonging, of being shaped by your city, and of nostalgia as a source of happiness amid the melancholy. 'I'd head into the back streets of Beyoğlu,' he wrote, 'and when I had reached Çurkurcuma, Galata, Cihangir, I would pause to gaze at the halos of the streetlamps and the light from a nearby television screen flickering on the wet pavements and it would be while peering into a junk shop, a refrigerator that an ordinary grocer used as a window display, a pharmacy still displaying a mannequin I remember from my childhood, that I would realise how very happy I was.'

Many foreign authors have viewed the city through a very different prism, that of the exotic. For them, Istanbul is a flamboyant city, where sultans kept harems and the bazaars are filled with the riches of the world; or it is a city of intrigue, an east–west crossroads and centre of espionage. And for most (but not all), it is a city of extraordinary beauty, a feeling shared with many Turkish writers.

This itinerary will explore the hotels, restaurants, buildings and other locations that have inspired authors. Among them are Agatha Christie, Mark Twain, Flaubert (who was more concerned about his syphilis than sightseeing), Knut Hamsun, Graham Greene, Gérard de Nerval and Turkish poet Yahya Kemal.

We start our Istanbul journey where so many others have: **Sirkeci Station** (see p71) in Eminönü, south of the Golden Horn. It's here that the Orient Express first rolled into Stamboul in October 1883. A byword for glamour, the Orient Express existed in several versions on various routes, most famously Paris-Vienna-Budapest-Istanbul. Between the Western 'city of light' and the shimmering Eastern exoticism of its ultimate destination, the train passed through a patchwork of mercurial Balkan kingdoms, always tinged with the promise of war or revolution. The cabins were decked out with damask drapes and silk sheets for the fold-down beds and the saloon had leather armchairs and bookcases. Meals were served beneath gas-lit brass chandeliers at tables set with Baccarat crystal, starched napery and monogrammed porcelain. The kind of passengers who could afford all this tended to

be minor royals, wealthy nobility, diplomats and financiers, not to mention spies, nightclub performers and high-class whores – the perfect cast list for thriller-writers such as Agatha Christie, Ian Fleming and Graham Greene, each of whom used the Express as a setting for their novels *Murder on the Orient Express*, *From Russia With Love* and *Stamboul Train* respectively.

Within the station today, there is little of the glamour and intrigue of the days of the Orient Express. The original **Orient Express** restaurant (see p75), where Agatha Christie once ate, remains, and there is a new railway museum in the station, with one of the train's original tea services.

The final stop for Orient Express travellers was the **Pera Palace Hotel** (see box p137). From here, you can follow the route passengers would have once travelled – in sedan chairs – up to the hotel. Alternatively, reach the hotel by taking the funicular from the south side of Galata Bridge to Tünel Square. Walk across the square and along Sofyalı Sokak and then left at Asmalımescit Sokak. The hotel claims that Agatha Christie wrote her famous book in room 411. If it's not occupied, ask to look around; it has a library of her books and closely resembles what it would have looked like around the time of her stay.

Among the many distinguished guests to have stayed at the Pera Palace (including Queen Elizabeth II and Alfred Hitchcock) was controversial Norwegian writer and winner of the Nobel Prize in Literature Knut Hamsun. He wrote in 1889 about the view from the hotel: 'The sun that suddenly rises behind the hills of Pera, over the minarets of the city and the Golden Horn, fills your heart with a crimson joy.' To enjoy this view,

ITINERARIES

climb up to the small café by the car park above the Pera Palace.

Not all visitors, however, were so impressed with the city. In the middle of the 19th century the city began to receive its first proper 'tourists', drawn by the oriental mystique of the capital of the Ottoman sultans. Mark Twain was among them. He described his impressions in *Innocents Abroad*. Tourists dropped anchor in the Golden Horn and were rowed ashore to visit **Haghia Sophia** (see p54), which he described as 'the rustiest old barn in Heathendom'; see the Whirling Dervishes, which he reckoned were 'about as barbarous an exhibition as we have witnessed'; tour the **Grand Bazaar** (see p65): 'a monstrous hive of little shops'; and experience a hammam: 'a malignant swindle'. Twain was, however, fascinated by the beggars – the three-legged woman, the man with an eye in his cheek, the man with fingers on his elbow. His verdict? '*Bismillah!* The cripples of Europe are a delusion and a fraud. The truly gifted flourish only in the byways of Pera and Stamboul.'

To return to our tour, continue past the 'byways of Pera' to the Büyük Londra Hotel (see p142). This old hotel opened in 1892, three years before the Pera Palace. Today, it's become the kind of place the phrase 'faded glamour' was coined for. The bar is wonderfully eccentric, with a wind-up gramophone and parrots in cages. You can imagine the hotel's most illustrious guest, Ernest Hemingway, having a drink, or eight, here. He arrived on the Orient Express in 1922, aged just 23, to cover the Turkish War of Independence for the *Toronto Daily Star*. In his collection of articles, *In Our Time*, he wrote: 'In the morning when you wake and see a mist over the Golden Horn with the minarets rising out of it slim and clean

toward the sun and the muezzin calling the faithful to prayer in a voice that soars and dips like an aria from a Russian Opera, you have the magic of the East.'

From the hotel, turn right and then left on to Istiklal Caddesi. Pamuk has written about the visit of French poet and essayist Gérard de Nerval in 1843, remarking that Istiklal Caddesi probably looked 'almost the same as it does today', until you reach Taksim Square, which Nerval described as 'a vast, infinite pasture shaded by pine and nut trees'.

In *From Another Hill*, poet Yahya Kemal (1884-1958) wrote of Istanbul: 'There are many flourishing cities in the world/But you're the only one who creates enchanting beauty.' Walk back down Istiklal as far as Sakızağacı Caddesi to find the poet's regular haunt, **Hacı Abdullah Lokantası** (see p95), one of Istanbul's oldest restaurants and a favourite of many writers. Order meze and rakı, just like Kemal did.

Back on Istiklal, hop on the 'nostalgic' tram back to Tünel Square or take your time and browse the bookshops such as **Denizler Kitapevi** (see p96) or **Robinson Crusoe** (see p97). Once in Tünel Square, pause for a moment. This was the favourite viewpoint not only of Nerval, but also his close friend, the French poet Théophile Gautier, who once remarked: 'The view is so strangely beautiful that it seems unreal.' Much of that particular vista is now shrouded in concrete, but to get a good view, climb the **Galata Tower** (see p79) or walk down to **Galata Bridge** (see p72), from where the Istanbul of two continents opens before you. French writer and poet Alphonse de Lamartine (1790-1869) was inspired to say, 'If one had but a single glance to give the world, one should gaze on Istanbul'.

Istanbul by Area

Haghia Sophia p54

South of the Golden Horn

Sultanahmet and the adjacent districts south of the Golden Horn comprise the 'proper' Istanbul: the one with the slim minarets pointing skywards and the domes – the 'Orient' of the Turkish Delight ad. It's a scenic thumbnail of land surrounded by sea on three sides, home to world-famous sites, among them the former church (then a mosque and now a museum) of **Haghia Sophia** and the **Topkapı Palace** complex, epicentre of the Ottoman Empire. These, along with other mosques, museums and assorted historical oddments, are testament to a heritage that encompasses the birth, youthful exuberance, mature middle age and drooling dotage of not one, but two, great empires: Byzantine and Ottoman. And despite the number of tourists

who come to explore the area today, its 1,500-year history of power remains as palpable as ever.

Topkapı Palace

Directly behind Haghia Sophia are the walls shielding the Topkapı Palace complex. Part command centre for a massive military empire, part archetypal Eastern pleasure dome, the palace was the hub of Ottoman power for over three centuries, until it was superseded by Dolmabahçe Palace in 1853. For lavish decor and exquisite location, it rivals Granada's Alhambra. At least half a day is needed to explore Topkapı; given the high entrance fee you might want to take a full day to get your money's worth. If you're pushed for time, the must-see features are the Harem (although there's an extra charge), Imperial Treasury and the views from the innermost courtyard. Be warned that any part of the palace may be closed at any time.

Sights & museums

Topkapı Palace
Topkapı Sarayı

Bab-ı Hümayün Caddesi (0212 512 0480, www.topkapisarayi.gov.tr). Tram Gülhane or Sultanahmet. **Open** *May-Sept* 9am-7pm Mon, Wed-Sun. *Oct-Apr* 9am-4pm Mon, Wed-Sun. **Admission** YTL20. *Harem* YTL15. **Map** p51 F3 ❶

The entrance to the palace is via the Imperial Gate (Bab-ı Hümayün), erected by the Sultan Fatih in 1478 and decorated with niches that during Ottoman times were used to display the severed heads of rebels and criminals. The gate leads into the first of a series of four courts, which become more private the deeper into the complex you penetrate.

The First Court was public and not considered part of the palace proper. It housed a hospital and dormitories for the palace guards, hence the popular name, Court of the Janissaries. Off to the left is the church of Haghia Irene (Aya Irini Kilisesi), built by Emperor Justinian and a contemporary of Haghia Sophia. It is the only pre-Ottoman conquest church in the city that was never turned into a mosque. Closed most of the time, the church serves as a concert venue during the International Istanbul Music Festival.

Still in the First Court, down the hill to the left, is the superb Archaeology Museum (see p53), but the palace proper is entered through the Disneyesque gate ahead. Tickets can be bought just before you reach the gate.

The Second Court

A semi-public space, the enormous Second Court is where the business of running the empire was carried out.

This is where the viziers of the imperial council sat in session in the divan, overlooking gardens landscaped with cypresses, plane trees and rose bushes. Where once there would have been crowds of petitioners awaiting their turn for an audience, nowadays there are queues to get in to the Harem, an introverted complex of some 300 brilliantly tiled chambers on several levels, connected by arcaded courts and fountain gardens. Unfortunately, access is limited: you must wait to join a group that leaves every half-hour and is led through no more than a dozen chambers by an official guide. It's not the ideal way to see the place – but it's the only way. Tickets are sold separately (YTL15), from a window located beside the Harem entrance.

Around from the Harem ticket window, a low brick building topped by shallow domes is the former State Treasury, present home of an exhibition of arms and armour. (Note the contrast between cumbersome, bludgeonly European swords and the lighter Ottoman model.)

Across the gardens, a long row of ventilation chimneys punctuates the roof line of the enormous kitchens, which catered for up to 5,000 inhabitants of the palace. They contain a collection of ceramics, glass and silverware, much of it imported from China and Japan via Central Asia, along the legendary Silk Route. The earliest pieces are Chinese celadon, particularly valued by the sultans because it was supposed to change colour when brought into contact with poison.

All paths in the Second Court converge on the Gate of Felicity (Bab-üs Saadet), the backdrop for an annual performance of Mozart's *Abduction from the Seraglio*. The gate also gives access to the Third Court.

The Third Court

The Third Court was the sultan's own private domain. Confronting all who enter is the Audience Chamber (Arz

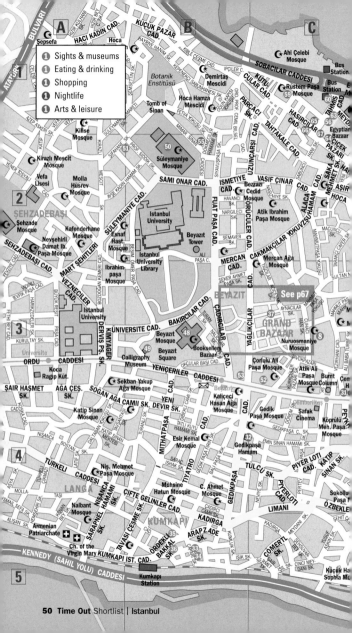

Legend:
1 Sights & museums
2 Eating & drinking
3 Shopping
4 Nightlife
5 Arts & leisure

South of the Golden Horn

Emirönü-Besiktas

Karaköy-Haydarpasa-Kadiköy

Sirkeci Görem (Araba ...

Istanbul-Marmara-Akdeniz Hatti

Atatürk Statue

Seraglio Point

KENNEDY CADDESI

REŞADIYE CADDESI

YALI KÖŞKÜ SK.

EMINÖNÜ

MIMAR

HAMIDIYE CAD.

KEMALETTIN CAD.

Sirkeci

SIRKECI ISTASYON CADDESI

ANKARA CAD.

Sirkeci Station
32

Goths Column

ŞAH PEHLEVI

ISTASYON ARKASI SK.

NÖBETHANE CAD.

HATUN SK.

HÜDAVENDIGAR CAD.

2

ASIR EF. CAD.

MURADIYE CAD.

KEMAL

TAYA

Karakı Hüs. Çelebi Mosque

Gülhane Zoo

EBUSSUUT CAD.

IBMl

Gülhane Park

Bab-ı Ali Mosque

Tanzimat Museum

Istanbul Erek Lisesi

Istanbul Vilayet

HÜKÜMET KONAĞI SK.

61

Bab-ı Ali

Tiled Kiosk

Topkapı Palace
1

ÇAĞ CAD.

ANKARA

Cağaloğlu Hamam
21

Alay Köşkü

Archaeology Museum
2

TOPKAPI PALACE

Topkapı Palace Ticket Office

Aga Mosque

ALEMDAR CAD.

BABIALI CADDESI

PROF. K. ISMAIL GÜRKAN CAD.

Molla Fenari Mosque

ALAY KÖŞKÜ CAD.

Zeynep Sultan Mosque

Haghia Eirene

Konstantin Suru

Yerebatan Mosque

ZENEP SULTAN

Gülhane

SOĞUKÇEŞME SK.

KENNEDY (SAHIL YOLU)

3

ÇEŞME SK.

SULTANAHMET

CAFERIYE SK.

Haghia Sophia
4

Imperial Gate

CAD.

ÇATAL

DIVAN YOLU

İNCİLİ ÇAVUŞ SK.

16 24
18 17
13
1

Yerebatan Sarnıcı

Fountain of Ahmet III

BABIHÜMAYUN CAD.

Binbirdirek Cistern
3

SULTANAHMET SQUARE

22

i

ISHAK

Museum of Turkish & Islamic Art
7

Tomb of Sultan Ahmet I

MIMAR

KABASAKAL CAD.

Baths of Roxelana
29

Four Seasons Hotel
25

PAŞA CAD.

AT MEYDANI

DALBASTI SK.

Hippodrome

Sultanahmet Mosque

KENNEDY

Örme Sütun

10

Vakıflar Carpet Museum

20
6

Çankurtaran Station

Sea of Marmara
(Marmara Denizi)

SIFA HAMAMI

TAVUKHANE SK.

Mosaic Müseum

AYASOFYA CAD.

27

AKSAKAL SK.

NA KILBENT

AKSAKAL SK.

KENNEDY (SAHIL YOLU) CADDESI

400 m

400 yds

© Copyright Time Out Group 2010

Get the local experience

Over 50 of the world's top destinations available.

Odası), which is where foreign ambassadors would present their credentials, until the room's role was supplanted by the Sublime Porte. Although the sultan would be present on such occasions, he would never deign to speak with a non-Turk and all conversation was conducted via the grand vizier.

To the right is the Hall of Campaign Pages (Seferli Koşusu), whose task it was to look after the royal wardrobe. They certainly did an excellent job: there's a perfectly preserved 550-year-old, red and gold silk kaftan worn by Mehmet II, conqueror of Constantinople.

Things get even more glittery next door in the Imperial Treasury (Hazine). Many of the items here were made specifically for the palace by a team of court artisans, which at its height numbered over 600. A lot of what's displayed here has never left the confines of the inner courts. Not that too many people outside the sultan's circle would have had much use for a diamond-encrusted set of chain mail or a Qu'ran bound in jade. Items like the Topkapı Dagger, its handle set with three eyeball-sized emeralds (one of which conceals a watch face), are breathtaking in their excessiveness.

More remarkable still are the items in the Privy Chamber, which houses the Chamber of Sacred Relics. To the sound of the Qu'ran being read live, vistors trail around a series of items including Moses' staff and Muhammad's sword, tooth, beard and cloak.

The Fourth Court

The final and Fourth Court is a garden with stepped terraces leading towards Seraglio Point, the protruberance of land that watches over the entrance to the Golden Horn. Buildings are limited to a bunch of reasonably restrained pavilions, while the views over the Bosphorus are wonderful, as are the sea breezes on a sun-beaten summer's day. Most notable is the Baghdad Kiosk, built to celebrate Murad IV's Baghdad Campaign in 1638, its glimmering

mother-of-pearl furniture is remarkable. The very last building to be constructed within the palace, the Mecidiye Pavilion (Mecidiye Köşkü), built in 1840, now houses a restaurant and café, notable for its enviable terrace seating.

Archaeology Museum, Tiled Pavilion & Museum of the Ancient Orient

Osman Hamdi Bey Yokuşu, Topkapı Sarayı (0212 520 7740). Tram Gülhane. **Open** 9am-5pm Tue-Sun. **Admission** (incl Museum of the Ancient Orient & Tiled Pavilion) YTL10 . **Map** p51 E3 ❷

The collection of classical antiquities displayed here is world-class, although many of the galleries are looking a little tired. Greeting visitors is a grinning statue of Bes, a demonic Cypriot demigod of inexhaustible power and strength, qualities required of anyone hoping to get through even a fraction of the 20 galleries within. Starting with the pre-classical world, they cover 5,000 years of history, with artefacts gathered from all over Turkey and the Near East and grouped thematically. Highlights include a collection of sixth- to fourth-century BC sarcophagi from a royal necropolis at Sidon, in modern Lebanon.

Up on the first floor, Istanbul Through the Ages is a summary of the city's history presented through a few key pieces, including a serpent's head lopped off the column in the Hippodrome and a section of the iron chain that stretched across the Bosphorus to bar the way of invaders. One great innovation is a small children's area, complete with low cabinets.

The Tiled Pavilion (Çinili Köşk)

Across from the museum stands the Tiled Pavilion (Çinili Köşk), which dates back to 1472 and the reign of Sultan Mehmet II, Ottoman conqueror of Constantinople. Built in a Persian style, the pavilion displays some outstanding samples of Turkish tiles and ceramics from the Seljuk and

Ottoman periods, dating from between the end of the 12th century and the beginning of the 20th century.

Museum of the Ancient Orient

The Museum of the Ancient Orient contains antiquities from the Hittite , Mesopotamian and Egyptian cultures, including some wonderful monumental glazed-brick friezes from the main Ishtar Gate of sixth-century Babylon. There is also the world's first peace treaty (1283 BC), a clay tablet signed by the Hittite king Hattushilish III and Egyptian pharaoh Rameses II.

Sultanahmet

Focal point for disgorging tour buses and feeding ground for taxis, **Sultanahmet Square** is the obvious place to begin. Most of the city's major monuments are just a few minutes' walk from here, including the underground cistern **Yerebatan Sarnıcı**, **Sultanahmet Mosque** and the **Museum of Turkish & Islamic Art**.

Most notably, Sultanahmet Square acts as a forecourt to what for close to a thousand years was the greatest church in Eastern Christendom, the **Haghia Sophia**. To the south-west, a strip of over-touristy tea-houses and souvenir shops fringes the **Hippodrome** (At Meydanı), formerly the focal point of Byzantine Constantinople. At one time, this arena was used for races and ceremonies. It retains an odd assortment of monuments on the raised area around which chariots would have thundered. The **Egyptian obelisk** was removed from the Temple of Karnak in AD 390 by Emperor Theodosius. It was set upon a marble pedestal and carved with scenes of himself and his family at the races. Next to it is the bronze **Serpentine Column**, carried off from the Temple of Apollo at Delphi and installed here

by Constantine. Each of the three original serpent heads was decapitated over the years.

Overlooking the Hippodrome is the grand **Museum of Turkish and Islamic Art**, while down the hill from its south-west corner is the **Sokollu Mehmet Paşa Mosque**, another *tour de force* by Sinan.

Sights & museums

Binbirdirek Sarnıcı

Imran Ökten Sokak 4 (0212 518 1001, www.binbirdirek.com). Tram Sultanahmet. **Open** 9am-9pm daily. **Admission** YTL10. **Map** p51 D4 ❸
Like the more famous Yerebatan cistern, this one is a Byzantine forest of pillars and brick-vaulted ceilings, but sadly the restorers have put in a false floor that halves the original height of the chamber (a well at the centre illustrates the original floor level). No one has yet figured out what to do with the place and it currently unsuccessfully accommodates a couple of cafés, a bar and a restaurant. The admission fee gets you a free drink.

Haghia Sophia
Ayasofya Camii Müzesi

Sultanahmet Square (0212 522 1750). Tram Sultanahmet. **Open** 9am-5pm Tue-Sun, plus 1st Mon of every month. Galleries close 1hr earlier. **Admission** YTL20. **Map** p51 E4 ❹
The third sacred building on the site to bear the name, the existing Haghia Sophia ('Divine Wisdom') was dedicated on 26 December AD 537 by Emperor Justinian. Approached by a grand colonnaded avenue beginning at the city gates, Justinian's cathedral towered over all else and was topped by the largest dome ever constructed – a record it held until just over a thousand years later with Michelangelo's dome for St Peter's (1590). Adding to the wonder, the church served as a vast reliquary, housing a pilgrim's delight of biblical treasures.

Hubbly Bubbly

Put this in your pipe and smoke it.

Waterpipe, hookah, or 'hubbly-bubbly'. Call it what you will, Turks have been smoking the narghile since the early 17th century, despite religious authorities periodically denouncing the practice and calling for it to be banned. The tyrannical Murat IV (1623-40) decreed that anyone caught having so much as a quick puff should be sentenced to death.

In the late 19th and early 20th century, narghile smoking was all the rage in high society, particularly among women. That fad passed and in republican Istanbul the narghile was relegated to a pastime of the peasantry. But today, in the 21st century, it has become popular among students – and tourists – once again.

Narghile tobacco is typically soaked in molasses or apple juice, giving it a slightly sweet flavour; but you can get it straight and strong by asking for *tömbeki*. Prices are around YTL5-YTL10 a pipe, which lasts a good hour or more. Contrary to popular misconception, hashish is not an option, nor, sadly, is the traditional Ottoman blend of opium, perfume and crushed pearls.

The best place to sample a narghile is on the nameless pedestrian strip by the American Pazarı, below the old cannon foundry at Tophane. At any time of day or night, there might be 300 to 400 people here, an extraordinary mix of students, couples and families, all belching forth great clouds of grey smoke.

In Sultanahmet, **Enjoyer Café** (see p61), one of the most touristy of the many narghile cafés on the pedestrianised street north of Divan Yolu, is a good bet if you avoid the fruity tobaccos.

In the courtyard of an Ottoman seminary, the low tables and benches at **Erenler Çay Bahçesi** (see p70) are shaded with ivy-hung trellises. But perhaps the most popular place for a smoke is **Meşale** (see p62), a sunken café beside an arcade of tourist shops; it's pleasant in the evenings when locals descend. There are nightly performances of Turkish classical music and dervish dancing shows on Friday, Saturday and Sunday between 8pm and 10pm.

All this was lost in 1204, when adventurers and freebooters on Western Christendom's Fourth Crusade, raised to liberate Jerusalem and the Holy Lands, decided they would be equally content with a treasure-grabbing raid on the luxurious capital of their Eastern brethren. At Haghia Sophia they ripped the place apart, carrying off everything they could, and added insult to thievery by infamously placing a prostitute on the imperial throne.

Further destruction was narrowly avoided in 1453, when the Ottoman Turk armies, led by Mehmet II, breached the walls of the city of Constantinople and put its Byzantine defenders to flight. The church was converted into a mosque. During its time as a mosque the basilica acquired the addition of four minarets, from which to deliver the Muslim call to prayer. The construction of these minarets was staggered; only two are matching. In 1317, a series of unsightly buttresses was deemed necessary when the church seemed to be in danger of collapse. These aside, what you see today is essentially the church exactly as it was in Justinian's time.

At the death of the Ottoman Empire, with plans afoot to partition Istanbul along national lines, both the Greeks (on behalf of the Eastern Church) and the Italians (on behalf of the Western Church) lobbied for Haghia Sophia to be handed over to them. An expedient solution was effected in 1934 by the leaders of the new Turkish republic, who deconsecrated the building and declared it a museum.

At least the cathedral's interior remains impressive, particularly the main chamber with its fabulous dome, 30m (98ft) in diameter. The other extraordinary interior features are the mosaics. Plastered over by the conquering Ottomans, they were only rediscovered during renovations in the mid 19th century. Some of the best decorate the outer and inner narthexes, the long, vaulted chambers inside the present

main entrance. The non-figurative geometrical and floral designs are the earliest and date from the reign of Justinian. Further mosaics adorn the galleries, reached by a stone ramp at the northern end of the inner narthex.

At the eastern end of the south gallery, just to the right of the apse, is a glimmering representation of Christ flanked by the famous 11th-century empress, Zoe, and her third husband, Constantine IX. One of the few women to rule Byzantium, Zoe married late and was a virgin until the age of 50. She must have developed a taste for what she discovered, proceeding to go through a succession of husbands and lovers in the years left to her. On the mosaic in question, the heads and inscriptions show signs of being altered, possibly in an attempt to keep up with her active love life.

Küçük Haghia Sophia Mosque
Küçük Ayasofya Camii
Küçük Ayasofya Caddesi. Tram Sultanahmet. **Open** prayer times daily. **Admission** free. **Map** p50 C5 ❺

Also known as 'Little Haghia Sophia' because of its resemblance to Justinian's great cathedral. Like its larger namesake, it was originally a church. Also like its namesake, it's not much to look at from the outside, but possesses a fine interior, including a frieze honouring Justinian and his wife, Theodora. There's also a very pleasant garden, which has an adjoining café.

Mosaic Museum
Büyüksaray Mozaik Müzesi
Arasta Çarşısı, Torun Sokak 103 (0212 518 1205). Tram Sultanahmet. **Open** *Winter* 9am-5pm Tue-Sun. *Summer* 9am-7pm Tue-Sun. **Admission** YTL8. No credit cards. **Map** p51 D5 ❻

Behind Sultanahmet Mosque and slightly down the hill towards the Marmara is a small, 17th-century shopping street, built to provide rental

Sultanahmet Mosque p59

revenue for the upkeep of the mosque. It has been converted into a cluster of tourist shops, known as the Arasta Bazaar. Leading off here is a prefabricated hut that is the unlikely home of a fantastic archaeological find. Uncovered in the mid 1950s, it's an ornamental pavement belonging to the Byzantine Great Palace (Büyüksaray), which stood where the mosque is now, and probably dates from the era of Justinian. The surviving segments depict mythological and hunting scenes, with pastoral idylls disturbingly skewed by bloody depictions of animal combat: elephant versus lion, snake versus gazelle, stags and lizards being eaten by winged unicorns. The museum is also worth a visit for the informative wall panels, particularly the pictorial reconstructions of how the Byzantine palace quarter would have looked.

Museum of Turkish & Islamic Art
Türk ve Islam Eserleri Müzesi
At Meydanı 46 (0212 518 1805). Tram Sultanahmet. **Open** 9am-6.30pm Tue-Sun. **Admission** YTL10. **Map** p51 D4 **7**

Overlooking the Hippodrome, the museum occupies the restored 16th-century palace of Ibrahim Paşa. A Greek convert to Islam, Ibrahim was the confidant of Süleyman I and in 1523 he was appointed Grand Vizier. When his palace was completed the following year, it was the grandest private residence in the Ottoman Empire, rivalling any building of the Topkapı Palace.

The palace was seized by the state and was variously used as a school, a dormitory, a court, a barracks and a prison, before being restored as a museum. The well-planned collections, all housed in cool rooms around a central courtyard, include carpets, manuscripts, miniatures, woodwork, metalwork and glasswork. Items date from the early Islamic period through

to modern times, all presented chronologically and geographically, with full explanations provided.

On the ground floor, a gallery showcases modern Turkish and foreign artists. There's an interesting ethnographic section, including a recreation of a *kara çadır* or 'black tent', the residence of choice for many of the nomadic Anatolian tribes who developed the art of the *kilim*. Upstairs, the Great Hall contains what is reckoned to be one of the finest collections of carpets in the world. There's an excellent café in a shaded courtyard, with a covered terrace overlooking the Hippodrome next to it.

Nuruosmaniye Mosque
Nuruosmaniye Camii
Vezirhanı Caddesi (0212 528 0906). Tram Beyazıt or Çemberlitaş. **Open** 10am-7pm daily. **Admission** free. **Map** p50 C3 **8**

Constructed on one of the seven hills within the walls of the former Constantinople, this was the first mosque in the city built in the style known as Turkish Baroque. Istanbul historian John Freely describes the architecture as possessing a 'certain perverse genius'. Certainly, the courtyard shaded by plane trees is lovely. The extensive manuscript library is also worth a look.

Sokollu Mehmet Paşa Mosque
Sokollu Mehmet Paşa Camii
Şehit Mehmet Paşa Sokak 20 (0212 518 1633). Tram Eminönü or Sultanahmet. **Open** 7am-dusk daily. **Admission** free. **Map** p50 C5 **9**

One of Sinan's later buildings (constructed between 1571-72), this mosque has been widely praised by architectural historians for its skilful handling of an uneven, sloping site. If you manage to get inside (hang around long enough, and somebody will usually turn up with a key), notice the lovely tiling and painted calligraphic inscriptions, set among vivid floral motifs. If you don't, the ornate ablution fountain in the courtyard is also beautiful.

Sultanahmet (Blue) Mosque
Sultanahmet Camii
Meydanı Sokak 17 (0212 518 1319).
Tram Sultanahmet. **Open** 9am-1hr before dusk (prayer time) daily.
Admission free. **Map** p51 D4 ⓾
Seductively curvaceous and enhanced by a lovingly attended park in front, Sultanahmet Mosque is Islamic architecture at its sexiest. Commissioned by Sultan Ahmet I (1603-17) and built for him by Mehmet Ağa, a student of Sinan, this was the last of Istanbul's magnificent imperial mosques, the final flourish before the rot set in. It provoked hostility at the time because of its six minarets – such a display was previously reserved only for the Prophet's mosque at Mecca – but they do make for a beautifully elegant silhouette, particularly gorgeous when floodlit at night.

By contrast, the interior is clumsy, marred by four immense pillars, disproportionately large for the fairly modest dome they support (especially when compared to the vast yet seemingly unsupported dome that caps Haghia Sophia). Most surfaces are covered by a mismatch of Iznik tiles: their colour gives the place its popular name, the Blue Mosque.

In the north-east corner of the surrounding park is the *türbe* or tomb of Sultan Ahmet I. The mausoleum also contains the cenotaphs of his wife and three of his sons, two of whom, Osman II and Murat IV, ruled in their turn, Ahmet being the sultan who abandoned the nasty Ottoman practice of strangling other potential heirs on the succession of the favoured son.

Theodosius Cistern
Şerefiye Sarnıcı
Piyer Loti Caddesi. Tram Sultanahmet.
Open 9am-5pm Mon-Fri. **Admission** free. **Map** p50 C4 ⓫

This unrestored Byzantine reservoir is what the more famous Yerebatan Sarnıçı would have looked like before it was cleaned up for the tourists.

Tomb of Mahmut II
Mollafenari Mehallesi, 82 Divan Yolu.
Tram Sultanahmet. **Open** 9.30am-7pm daily. **Admission** free. **Map** p51 D4 ⓬
Mahmut II (1808-39) was the sultan who crushed the Janissaries, the Ottomans' elite standing army. He must have been a formidable force in the harem, too, producing 15 sons and 12 daughters, many of whom are now crammed into the domed tomb with him.

Yerebatan Sarnıcı
Yerebatan Caddesi 13 (0212 522 1259, www.yerebatan.com). Tram Sultanahmet. **Open** 9am-8pm daily.
Admission YTL10. **Map** p51 E4 ⓭
Built by the Emperor Justinian at the same time as the Haghia Sophia, this cistern was forgotten for centuries and only rediscovered by a Frenchman, Peter Gyllius in 1545 when he noticed that people got water by lowering buckets through holes in their basements. It's a tremendous engineering feat, with brick vaults supported on 336 columns spaced at four-metre (13-foot) intervals. Prior to restoration in 1987, the cistern could only be explored by boat (James Bond rowed through in *From Russia With Love*). These days there are concrete walkways. The subdued lighting and subterranean cool are especially welcome on hot days. Look for the two Medusa heads at the far end from the entrance, both recycled from an even more ancient building and casually employed as column bases. There's a café down here and a platform on which occasional concerts of classical music are performed.

Eating & drinking

Big on sights it may be, but Sultanahmet is still woefully underserved by decent restaurants and

Hammam hints

Top tips in navigating a Turkish bath.

Paying a burly, near-naked stranger to scrape, knead and pummel your flesh as you lie on a steamy slab of marble is one of Istanbul's hedonistic highlights. Although the process can appear daunting, most hammams are used to slightly bemused-looking visitors. For an introduction, many hotels have a version of a hammam, but make the effort to visit a real one. After all, as British novelist Maggie O'Farrell put it: 'If heaven exists, I hope it's a hammam.'

Lengthy menus offer such treats as massage, depilation and pedicures, but it boils down to whether you just want to look after yourself, or whether you want to pay extra for the services of a masseur (who'll also give you a good soaping and scrub).

Once you've paid, you enter the *camekan*, a kind of reception area. Some of these are splendid affairs with several storeys of wooden cubicles and a gurgling central fountain. This is where you get changed. You will be given a colourful checked cloth, known as a *peştemal*, to be tied around the waist for modesty. Keep this on at all times – it's bad form to flash. Both sexes also get *takunya*, wooden clogs that can be lethal on wet marble floors. Plastic slippers are often substituted nowadays.

A door from the *camekan* leads through to the *soğukluk*, which is for cooling off and has showers and toilets; another leads into the *hararet*, or steam room. These can be plain or ornate, but are nearly always covered in marble and feature a great dome inset with star-shaped coloured glass admitting a soft, diffuse light. Billowing clouds of steam fog the air.

There are no pools, as Muslims traditionally consider still water to be unclean. Instead, the *hararet* is dominated by a great marble slab known as the *göbektaşı* or 'navel stone'. Here, customers lie and sizzle like eggs on a skillet.

The most tourist-friendly hammams include **Çemberlitaş** and **Cağaloğlu** (for both, see p64), and **Süleymaniye** (see p71).

bars. It would be unfair to say that all the eateries are tourist traps, but it wouldn't be far off the mark. Below are a few exceptions.

Amedros

Hoca Rüstem Sokak 7, off Divan Yolu (0212 522 8356). Tram Sultanahmet. **Open** 11am-1am daily. **$$. Turkish.** **Map** p51 D3 ⑭
Though it's a European-style bistro, Amedros also does good Ottoman dishes. The house special is *testi kebabı*, lamb roasted with vegetables in a sealed clay pot that is cracked open at the table. In summer, candlelit tables are lined up in the cobbled alley; in winter, diners are warmed by a crackling fire.

Balıkçı Sabahattin

Seyit Hasan Kuyu Sokak 1, off Cankurtaran Caddesi (0212 458 1824, www.balikcisabahattin.com). Tram Sultanahmet. **Open** 11am-12.30am daily. **$$$. Seafood. Map** p51 E4 ⑮
Most visitors who are staying around Sultanahmet head to Kumkapı for fish, unaware that there's a far better option on their doorstep. It benefits from a gorgeous setting: a street of picturesque old wooden houses, periodically rattled to their foundations by the commuter trains passing in and out of Sirkeci. There's no menu: instead, bow-tied waiters present you with a tray of various meze and, later, a huge iced platter of seasonal fish and seafood from which to choose. Entertainment comes in the form of skittering cats skilled at doleful looks and pleading meows. Reservations are essential.

Djazzu

NEW *Alemdar Mahallesi, Incili Çavuş Çıkmazı 5-7 (0212 512 2242). Tram Sultanahmet.* **Open** 11am-1.30am daily. **$$. Modern European.** **Map** p51 D4 ⑯
In a small alleyway by Şah Bar, just off Incili Çavuş Sokak, Djazzu's attractive

pavement seating area and interior beat its considerable competition in the design stakes. The menu is also a gear above the usual Turkish cuisine of the area, with a fusion, Mediterranean-influenced menu cooked by a Japanese chef: the marinated *maguro* (tuna) is particularly good. There's also a good selection of Turkish wines.

Dubb Indian Restaurant

Alemdar Mahallesi, Incili Çavuş Sokak 10 (0212 513 7308, www.dubb indian.com). Tram Sultanahmet. **Open** noon-11pm daily. **$$. Indian.** **Map** p51 D4 ⑰
Istanbul is not exactly brimming with Indian restaurants, and this little gem in the heart of Sultanahmet might be the closest you'll get to eating authentic dishes from the subcontinent. There's a wide variety of curries, thalis and dishes from the *tandoor*, along with Indian drinks like salty or sweet lassi. All the bread is baked in house daily. There's a set menu at YTL36. The roof terrace – up seemingly endless flights of stairs – is worth the climb.

Enjoyer Café

Incili Çavuş Sokak 25 (0212 512 8759). Tram Sultanahmet. **Open** 9am-2am daily. **Narghile café.** **Map** p51 D4 ⑱
See box p55.

Fes Café

Ali Baba Türbe Sokak 25-27 (0212 526 3071). Tram Çemberlitaş. **Open** 9am-9pm daily. **Café. Map** p50 C3 ⑲
Located on a quiet street near the Nuruosmaniye Mosque, just off Nuruosmaniye Caddesi, this café's modern design blends surprisingly well with its antiquated surroundings. With a sister establishment smack in the centre of the Grand Bazaar, Fes Café is something of a local institution. The fresh-pressed lemonade and mint tea are both refreshing after a heavy shopping session. Be sure to check out

ISTANBUL BY AREA

Abdullah, a little shop in the café that sells gorgeous natural textiles, plus an assortment of olive oil-based soaps. There's another branch inside the Grand Bazaar.

Meşale

Arasta Bazaar 45 (0212 518 9562). **Open** 24 hours daily. *Tram Sultanahmet.* **Narghile café.** Map p51 D5 ⏨
See box p55.

Mozaik

Divanyolu Caddesi, Incili Çavuş Sokak 1 (0212 512 4177). Tram Sultanahmet. **Open** *Restaurant* 9am-midnight daily. *Bar* 9am-2am daily. **$$. Turkish.** Map p51 D4 ⏨

A cut above many of Sultanahmet's more slapdash establishments. When it is too chilly to sit at the pavement tables, the interior, with wooden floors carpeted with old kilims, copper platters and creaking stairs between the restaurant's three floors, offer romantic potential for dinner à deux. The international menu covers a lot of ground – everything from chicken mandarin to T-bone steak – but the special is *abant kebap*, a spectacular West Anatolian dish. After dinner, head for the basement bar.

Pudding Shop

Divanyolu Caddesi 6 (0212 522 2970, www.puddingshop.com). Tram Sultanahmet. **Open** 7am-11pm daily. **$. Turkish.** Map p51 D4 ⏨

A landmark in hippie history. In the pre-*Lonely Planet* days of the late 1960s and early 1970s, the Pudding Shop (founded 1957) was a bottleneck for all the overland traffic passing through on its tie-dyed, spliff-addled way east to Kathmandu. In addition to the food, the place served up travel information – courtesy of the two brothers who owned it, a busy bulletin board, and the like-minded company. It even crops up in the movie *Midnight Express.* Smartened up for the 21st-century tourist – plate-glass windows, gleaming display cabinets and slick staff – the restaurant still doles out basic canteen-style fare, no better or worse than half a dozen similar restaurants along this strip.

Rumeli

Ticarethane Sokak 8, off Divanyolu Caddesi (0212 512 0008). Tram Sultanahmet. **Open** 9am-midnight daily. **$$. Modern Turkish.** Map p51 D4 ⏨

Rumeli's food is far superior to the tourist fodder served at the the cluster of establishments at the bottom of Divan Yolu. A former printworks with a cavernous interior of exposed brick, stone and stained floorboards, it rises several floors from the cobbled side-street up to the roof terrace. Traditional Ottoman dishes are given a Mediterranean twist, along with excellent salads, pasta, and a very decent wine list. There are dishes from the Kurdish and Armenian regions too. Staff are charming.

Şah Bar

Alemdar Mahallesi, Incili Çavuş Çıkmazı (0212 519 5807). Tram Sultanahmet. **Open** noon-2am daily. **Bar.** Map p51 D4 ⏨

This is a true drinking bar, with loud Western music, Efes flowing and a rowdy backpacker crowd. It's something rare in Sultanahmet, and welcome for that. There are some snacks, but it's best to visit after dinner elsewhere for drinking into the night and singing along to soul classics.

Seasons Restaurant

Four Seasons Hotel, Tevfikhane Sokak 1 (0212 638 8200, www.fourseasons.com). Tram Sultahamet. **Open** noon-3pm, 7-11pm. **$$$$. Modern European.** Map p51 E4 ⏨

Still a high-end Sultanahmet establishment with an international menu, the Seasons Restaurant can't compare with the flair of newer restaurants like Ulus 29 (see p124), Topaz (see p104) and Mimolett (see p103). In a glass enclosure in the gardens of the Four Seasons Hotel, the restaurant aims at elegance – but the look is still very hotel-like, and diners are mainly tourists or hotel guests.

Yeşil Ev Beer Garden

Kabasakal Caddesi 5 (0212 517 6785). Tram Sultanahmet. **Open** 7am-11pm daily. **Bar.** Map p51 E4 ㉖

This idyllic garden of towering laurel, linden and horse chestnut trees belongs to the quaint Yeşil Ev guest-house. It's the finest place for an aperitif this side of the Golden Horn. In winter, guests are sheltered in a large conservatory amid hanging plants. Pricey, but worth it.

Shopping

Cocoon

Küçükayasofya Caddesi 13 & 17 (0212 638 6450, www.cocoontr.com). Tram Sultanahmet. **Open** 8.30am-7pm Mon-Sat. Map p51 D5 ㉗

See box right.

Galeri Kayseri

Divan Yolu 58 (0212 512 0456, www.galerikayseri.com). Tram Sultanahmet. **Open** 9am-8.30pm daily. Map p51 D4 ㉘

This shop is devoted exclusively to books about Istanbul and Turkey. Whatever the genre, you'll find it here: fiction, non-fiction, guidebooks and coffee-table volumes.

Istanbul Handicrafts Centre

Kabasakal Caddesi 5 (0212 517 6784/8). Tram Sultanahmet. **Open** 9am-6.30pm daily. Map p51 E4 ㉙

The Istanbul Handicrafts Centre is located in a restored *medrese* (religious school), opposite the Baths of Roxelana. It now houses a warren of workshops, each with its own specialisation. The most accomplished handicrafts are

The mad hatter

The shop that is reinventing the fez.

Cocoon (see left) is an astonishingly colourful store. Hundreds of hats cover the walls and fill the window. Some have bobbles, some have bells; one, yellow and black, looks like a bee. Each is unique.

It's a shop that screams fun. Using needle felting and knitting methods, these hats are all made in Turkey to designs by owner Seref Özen. You might not want to wear all of them to the pub, perhaps, but if nothing else, they'll certainly be a talking point. And some of them are subtle enough to wear anywhere.

Alongside the hats, the shop – over four floors in the shadow of Sultanahmet Mosque – stocks necklaces, earrings, hammam wear, shirts, trousers, brooches and wall hangings. It's the perfect souvenir shop for the discerning visitor: ethical, fun, unique and reasonably priced.

Seref also owns another shop two doors down, which is a much more serious proposal. He is considered to be one of the foremost authorities in the world on Central Asian textiles and spends much of his time travelling the region sourcing antique *ikat* coats, hats, embroideries, flatweaves and, of course, rugs for the serious collector. Be sure to browse the museum-like shop, even if not buying. There is another branch in the Arasta Bazaar.

ISTANBUL BY AREA

the illuminated manuscripts, miniatures and calligraphy. Other highlights include cloth-painting, dolls, ceramics, glassware and hand-bound books. The artists work on site, so you can watch them at their trade.

Arts & leisure

Cağaloğlu Hamamı

Prof Kazım Ismail Gürkan Caddesi 34 (0212 522 2424, www.cagaloglu hamami.com.tr). Tram Gülhane or Sultanahmet. **Open** *Men* 8am-10pm daily. *Women* 8am-8pm daily. No credit cards. **Map** p51 D3 **③⓪**

More or less unchanged since it was built in 1741, Cağaloğlu – pronounced 'jaah-lo-loo' – is Istanbul's most famous hammam. It is often used as a backdrop for soap ads and pop videos. The two-storey *camekan* has a baroque fountain, while the grand *hararet* seems inspired by the domed chamber of an imperial mosque. Illustrious former bathers include Franz Liszt, Florence Nightingale and Tony Curtis.

Çemberlitaş Hamamı

Vezirhan Caddesi 8 (0212 522 7974, www.cemberlitashamami.com.tr). Tram Çemberlitaş. **Open** 6am-midnight daily. **Map** p51 C4 **③①**

Possibly the cleanest and most atmospheric hamam in town. Built in 1584 by Sinan, it was commissioned by Nurbanu, wife of Sultan Selim the Sot, as a charitable foundation for the poor. The hamam has been in continual use ever since. There are sections for both sexes, but part of the ladies' wing was torn down in the 19th century. Women now change in a corridor rather than a proper *camekan*, although the main *hararet* is lovely. Close to the Grand Bazaar, the hamam is frequented by foreigners; as a result, the masseurs are perfunctory and more interested in hassling for tips. But there's usually someone at reception who speaks English, and if you're a hamam virgin, this is a good place to begin.

Gedikpaşa Hamamı

Hamam Caddesi 65-7, off Gedikpaşa Caddesi (0212 517 8956). Tram Beyazıt. **Open** *Men* 6am-11.30pm daily. *Women* 9am-10.30pm daily. No credit cards. **Map** p50 B4 **③②**

One of Istanbul's oldest hamams, Gedikpaşa was built in 1457 by one of Mehmet the Conqueror's viziers, next door to the mosque that also bears his name. Although not in the same architectural league as the Çemberlitaş or Cağaloğlu, the interior remains largely intact. Both men's and women's sections are a little run-down but clean. The men's area includes a small pool and sauna.

Kumkapı

Situated inside the city walls on the Sea of Marmara coast, this former fishing port is now an inner-city neighbourhood of cobbled lanes lined with seafood restaurants, where persistent hawkers attempt to waylay passers-by. A shortish taxi ride from Sultanahmet, Kumkapı is not a bad choice for fresh fish, although the popular restaurants along **Çapari Sokak** have long been eclipsed by the *meyhanes* at Nevizade (see p100) and fancy fish places up the Bosphorus.

Eating & drinking

Of the 50 or so restaurants in Kumkapı. There are a few that locals rate highly, including **Akvaryum Fish Restaurant**, which has live *fasıl* music, as does **Çapari**, one of the district's oldest establishments. **Kartallar Balıkçı** is famous for its *balık çorbası* (fish chowder) and *buğulama* (steamed fish casserole) – and has a large celebrity quotient among its clientele. In business since 1938, **Kör Agop** is known for its top quality fish and *fasıl*.

Prices are conspicuously absent from menus, so make sure to agree on the bill in advance. Most places offer fixed meal deals, kicking off with meze followed by fish of the day and dessert. Expect to pay around YTL50 per person with alcohol (*rakı*, local wine or beer).

Fasıl musicians roam between the restaurants serenading outdoor diners, while an odd assortment of street vendors flog anything from fresh almonds to Cuban cigars.

Akvaryum Fish Restaurant
Çapari Sokak 39 (0212 517 2273). Kumkapı station. **Open** 10:30am-1am daily. **Seafood**. Map p50 B5 ㉝

Çapari
Çapari Sokak 22 (0212 517 7530, www.capari.net). Kumkapı station. **Open** 10am-2am daily. **Seafood**. Map p50 B5 ㉞

Kartallar Balıkçı
Capriz Sokak 32 (0212 517 2254, www.valentinokartallar.com). Kumkapı station. **Open** 10am-midnight daily. **Seafood**. Map p50 B5 ㉟

Kör Agop
Ördekli Bakkal Sokak 7 (0212 517 2334). Kumkapı station. **Open** noon-2am daily. **Seafood**. Map p50 B5 ㊱

Grand Bazaar

For centuries, this was where the strands of an empire's economy came together, with sellers from Damascus and Yemen bartering hard with buyers from Anatolia, the Balkans and the Aegean. A cacophony of multilingual haggling and braying camels, this was the oriental bazaar *par excellence*.

While nowadays the **Grand Bazaar** is given over to a more decorative tourist trade, the experience of shopping here can still be something of a contact sport, as shopkeepers try to sell a multitude of goods – ranging from the beautiful to the tacky – to visitors. Meanwhile, in the surrounding streets, Istanbul's masses still do the real business, descending on the markets to do their weekly shopping – the modern bazaar.

Sights & museums

Grand Bazaar
Kapalı Çarşı
0212 522 3173,www.kapalicarsi. com.tr. Tram Beyazıt or Çemberlitaş. **Open** 8.30am-7pm Mon-Sat. Map p50 C3 ㊲

The Grand Bazaar (in Turkish *Kapalı Çarşı*, or 'Covered Market') is a world apart. A maze of interconnecting vaulted passages, the bazaar has its own banks, baths, mosques, cafés and restaurants, a police station and post office, not to mention thousands of shops, all glittery and fairy-lit in the absence of natural light. Since the rise of the mall it's no longer the biggest shopping centre in the world, but it can still claim to be the oldest.

Part of the building dates back to the ninth century, when it was used as something akin to a Byzantine ministry of finance. Trading proper started in 1461, a mere eight years after the Turkish conquest of Constantinople. The Ottomans ushered in a new economic era, with the city at the centre of an empire that stretched from the Arabian deserts almost to the European Alps. Mehmet the Conqueror ordered the construction of a *bedesten*, a great secure building with thick stone walls, massive iron gates and space for several dozen shops. This survives in modified form as the Old Bedesten (*İç Bedesten*), at the very heart of the bazaar. It remains a place where the most precious items are sold, including the finest old silver and antiques. The Sandal Bedesten was added later; named after a fine Bursan silk, it was filled with textile traders. It now hosts a carpet auction at 1pm every Wednesday, which is a crowd-pleaser.

A network of covered streets grew up around the two *bedestens*, sealed at night behind 18 great gates. Whenever the economy was booming, the market would physically expand, only to be cut back by frequent fires. As the Ottoman Empire started to decline after 300 years of wealth, so did the legendary splendour of the bazaar. In 1894, a devastating earthquake hit the traders particularly hard. It wasn't until the 1950s that the bazaar began to revive, as the new republic found its economic footing. These days, it's taking tentative steps into the 21st century with chic boutiques, hip cafés, and even a website.

The bazaar definitely has plenty of inessential knick-knacks, tacky souvenirs, nasty leather jackets, hookah pipes and hippie outfits, but there are some attractive, unusual and high-quality goods to be had; you just have to know where to look and be prepared to haggle.

Eating & drinking

Divan
Kapalıçarşı Cevahir Bedesten 143-151 (0212 520 2250). Tram Beyazıt Kapalıçarşı. **Open** 9am-7pm Mon-Sat. **Café**. **Map** p67 B2 ❸
The Grand Bazaar has a few little places to stop for a *çay*, but there's one place in the Old Bazaar, or Cevahir Bedesten, that stands out. Divan is a simulated slice of the suave old days of the Republic, with burgundy walls, red leather couches, a huge Turkish flag draped from the ceiling, and a crystal chandelier beside a giant portrait of Atatürk. The extensive coffee menu, however, is up to date and features the likes of frappuccinos, plus decent sandwiches and sweets.

Shopping

Abdulla
Halıcılar Caddesi 53, Grand Bazaar (0212 522 3070, www.abdulla.com). Tram Beyazıt. **Open** 9am-7pm Mon-Sat. **Map** p67 B2 ❸
Abdulla is all about a contemporary take on traditional crafts. The bywords are 'natural' and 'handmade'; the main product line is hamam accessories, so you will find towels, *peştemals* and olive oil soaps in scents from cinnamon and tea to sesame. Other good buys include sheepskin throws and hand-spun silk and wool.

Ahmet Hazım
Takkeciler Caddesi 61-63, Grand Bazaar (0212 52 9886, www.ahmet hazim.com). Tram Beyazıt. **Open** 8.30am-7pm Mon-Sat. **Map** p67 B2 ❹
One of the oldest rug merchants in the bazaar, specialising in kilims and carpets from Turkey, Iran and the Caucasus and *suzanis* (embroidered textiles) from Uzbekistan. You get is quality service and none of the hard sell.

Antique Objet
Zenneciler Caddesi 48-50, Grand Bazaar (0212 526 7451, www.antique objet.com). Tram Beyazıt. **Open** 9am-7pm Mon-Sat. **Map** p67 B2 ❹
Crammed into an awkward space by the entrance to the market's İç Bedesten, this den of delights stocks own-label boots, Cinderella slippers and jackets in velvet Suzani cloth, sleek short coats of rich Ottoman fabric and a line of bags in *suzani* and *ikat*. Workmanship is top notch.

Deli Kızın Yeri
Halıcılar Caddesi 82, Grand Bazaar (0212 526 1251, www.delikiz.com). Tram Beyazıt. **Open** 8.30am-7pm Mon-Sat. **Map** p67 B2 ❹
Linda Caldwell, a retired American and self-styled crazy lady (*deli kız*) turns traditional Turkish handicrafts, motifs and fabrics into something more off-beat.

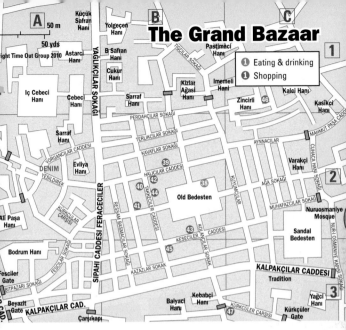

The Grand Bazaar

1 Eating & drinking
1 Shopping

Her unique designs include hand-made clothes, tablecloths, placemats and dolls.

Derviş

Keseciler Caddesi 33-35, Grand Bazaar (0212 514 4525, www.dervis.com). Tram Beyazıt. **Open** 9am-7pm Mon-Sat. **Map** p67 B2 **43**

Derviş nestles behind the narrowest of shop fronts. Here, Anatolian traditions are reinvented. Bathroom accessories are big, including handmade soaps in a host of natural flavours, super-soft unbleached cotton towels, and *peştemals* in linen, cotton and silk. But there are also shimmering scarves of hand-spun silk, felt slippers, rugs and throws, and mohair and patchwork fur blankets; plus brimming shelves of original dowry items, trawled from the depths of Anatolia by owner Tayfun Utkan. Look out for the hand-stitched bolero jackets, ethnic coats and dresses in fabulous colours and fabrics, and exquisitely embroidered linens.

Ethnicon

Kapalıçarşı Takkeciler Sokak 58-60, Grand Bazaar (0212 345 5620, www. ethnicon.com). Tram Beyazıt. **Open** 8.30am-7pm Mon-Sat. **Map** p67 B2 **44**

Ethnicon (short for 'ethnic contemporary') creates kilims with a modern twist. They are made without child labour and using environmentally friendly processes, so colours tend to be muted. Browsing in Ethnicon is a very different – and more peaceful – experience compared to the rest of the bazaar. Prices are fixed.

Kalender Carpets

Tekkeciler Caddesi 24-26, Grand Bazaar (0212 527 5518). Tram Beyazıt. **Open** 8.30am-7pm Mon-Sat. **Map** p67 B3 **45**

Kalender stocks a great collection of full-size, deep pile Anatolian carpets, which start from as little as YTL1,500. A good place to start your mission in 'carpet row', in the heart of the bazaar.

Kalender Carpets p67

Sisko Osman

*Zincirli Han 15, Grand Bazaar (0212
528 3548, www.siskoosman.com).
Tram Beyazıt.* **Open** 8.30am-6.30pm
Mon-Sat. **Map** p67 C1 ㊽

Sisko 'Fat Man' Osman is acknowl-
edged around the Grand Bazaar as the
leading authority on carpets and kilims. His well-stocked shop fills most of
the historic Zincirli Han, and his international clientele includes many well-
known people. So while you can be
sure of quality, don't expect a bargain.

Yörük

*Kürkçüler Çarşısı 16, Grand Bazaar
(0212 527 3211). Tram Beyazıt.* **Open**
8.30am-7pm Mon-Sat. **Map** p67 C3 ㊼

The shop may be tiny, but has some of
the finest treasures of the bazaar. You'll
find lots of kilims here, although the
real emphasis is on old ethnic rugs of
all sizes, mostly from the Caucasus.
Guide yourself towards Gürsel, one of
the dashing young partners, and you're
promised entertainment, little pressure
to buy and, quite probably, the rug of
your dreams.

Beyazıt

A large plaza west of the bazaar,
Beyazıt Square was the site of the
forum in Roman times. It regained
importance when the Ottomans
built a palace here, serving as the
pre-Topkapı seat of power until it
burned down in 1541. Significant
Ottoman structures still stand,
notably the **Beyazıt Mosque**.

Facing the mosque is the
monumental gate to **Istanbul
University**. In the 1960s and
1970s, the campus was a favourite
battleground for both left and right,
and is still a centre for political
protest. As a result, the university
grounds and **Beyazıt Tower**,
built in 1828 as a fire lookout and
a prominent city landmark, are
currently off limits to all but
accredited students.

Follow either of the roads that
hug the university walls to reach
the architectural perfection of the
Süleymaniye Mosque.

Sights & museums

Beyazıt Mosque
Beyazıt Camii

*Beyazıt Square, Yeniçeriler Caddesi.
Tram Beyazıt.* **Open** 10am-final
prayer call daily. **Admission** free.
Map p50 B3 ㊾

Built from 1501 to 1506, this was the
second great mosque complex to be
founded in the city. The first, the Fatih
Mosque, was destroyed, which makes
Beyazıt the oldest imperial mosque in
town. In effect, it's the architectural
link between the Byzantine Haghia
Sophia – the obvious inspiration – and
the great, later Ottoman mosques such
as Süleymaniye. The sultan for whom
it was built, Beyazıt II, is buried at the
back of the gardens. Still in use, the
mosque is full of market traders at
prayer times. Outside is the Sahaflar
Carsisi (book bazaar), where Sufi booksellers tout travelogues and novels in
many diffferent languages.

Calligraphy Museum
Vakıf Hat Sanatları Müzesi

*Beyazıt Square (0212 527 5851,
www.vgm.gov.tr). Tram Beyazıt.*
Museum currently closed for
renovations. **Map** p50 B3 ㊾

Forbidden to portray living beings by
religion (although this was not always
strictly adhered to), Islamic artists
developed alternative forms of virtuos-
ity. Calligraphy was regarded as a particularly noble art because it was a way
of beautifying the text of the Qu'ran.
But the sanctity of the text placed
restrictions on the flourishes that could
be added. Not so with the sultan's
tuğra, or monogram, which incorporated his name, titles and patronymics
into one highly stylised motif – the pre-
cursor of the modern logo. The tile
art here is excellent and there are a

number of brilliantly illuminated Qu'rans dating from the 13th to 16th centuries. The museum also has a pleasant courtyard that features stone-carved calligraphy. The Dar'ül-Kurra in the courtyard is accessible to visitors during museum opening hours in Ramadan; it contains some holy relics of the Prophet Muhammed.

At the time of going to press this museum was closed for much needed restoration and it's unclear when it will open again.

Süleymaniye Mosque
Süleymaniye Camii

Tiryakiler Çarşısı, off Prof Sıddık Sami Onar Caddesi. Tram Beyazıt or Eminönü. **Open** 9am-7pm daily. Closed for refurbishment until 2011. **Admission** free. **Map** p50 B2 (50)

Completed in 1557 under Süleyman the Magnificent, this stunning mosque is arguably the crowning achievement of architect Mimar Sinan. Built on Istanbul's highest hill, it is visible for miles. The low-rise, multi-domed buildings surrounding the mosque are part of its *külliye* (compound), and include a hospital, asylum, hamam and soup kitchen.

Walk through the gardens and arcaded courtyard, whose columns allegedly came from the Byzantine royal box at the Hippodrome, to enter the mosque – remarkable for its soaring central prayer room, illuminated by some 200 windows. The interior decoration is minimal but effective; it includes stained glass added by Ibrahim the Mad and sparing use of Iznik tiles (which Sinan would later use profusely at the Rüstem Pasha Mosque, just down the hill).

Behind the mosque are several *türbes* (tombs), including Süleyman's own beautifully restored grave. Haseki Hürrem, the sultan's influential wife, a former slave known as Roxelana, is buried beside him. Süleymaniye Mosque is closed until sometime in 2011 for major refurbishment.

Eating & drinking

Darüzziyafe

Şifahane Sokak 6 (0212 511 8414, www.daruzziyafe.com.tr). Tram Beyazıt, Eminönü or Laleli. **Open** noon-11pm daily. **$$$. Turkish.** **Map** p50 A2 (51)

The former soup kitchen of the Süleymaniye Mosque complex now turns out more varied fare. Although the menu runs to several pages, the food is still canteen cooking – great for lunch (and a favourite with tour buses) but too prosaic for dinner. The setting, a large courtyard filled with rose bushes and trees, is potentially lovely but rendered institutional by cheap furniture and neglect. The restaurant is located to the north of the mosque, separate from the row of small eateries which line its west side.

Erenler Çay Bahçesi

Çorlulu Ali Paşa Medresesi, Yeniçeriler Caddesi 36/28 (0212 528 3785). Tram Beyazıt. **Open** *Summer* 7am-3am daily. *Winter* 7am-midnight daily. No credit cards. **Narghile café.** **Map** p50 C3 (52)

See box p55.

Şar

Yeniceriler Caddesi 47 (0212 458 9219). Tram Beyazıt. **Open** 6am-11.30pm daily. **$. Turkish.** **Map** p50 B2 (53)

Among tourist restaurants south of the Golden Horn, this canteen stands as an island of Turkish food for Turkish people. The pick-and-point system also serves as a good introduction to the dishes. Pick your starter, main, salad, drink and dessert, pay and head upstairs. Şar has been here since 1957 and is known for its hearty food, such as the moussaka-like *gizli kebap* or the *pide çeşitleri*, a Turkish pizza. It's one of the cheaper options in the area. No alcohol. There is another, more upmarket, branch around the corner on Tiyatro Caddesi.

Shopping

Booksellers' Bazaar

Kapalı Çarşı (0212 522 3173, www.kapalicarsi.org.tr). Tram Beyazıt or Çemberlitaş. **Open** 8.30am-7pm Mon-Sat. **Map** p50 B3 54

West of Çadırcılar Caddesi, in Sahaflar Çarşısı Sokak, is the Booksellers' Bazaar, a lane and courtyard where the written word has been traded since early Ottoman times. Because printed books were considered a corrupting European influence, only hand-lettered manuscripts were sold until 1729, the year the first book in Turkish was published. Today, much of the trade at this historic bazaar is in textbooks (the university is nearby), along with plentiful coffee table volumes and framed calligraphy. Booksellers now have to compete with itinerant merchants peddling everything from Byzantine coins to used mobile phones.

Arts & leisure

Süleymaniye Hamamı

Mimar Sinan Caddesi 20 (0212 519 5569, www.suleymaniyehamami. com). Tram Eminönü. **Open** 10am-midnight daily. No credit cards. **Map** p50 B2 55

This hammam was built by the venerable Mimar Sinan in 1557. It was once part of a structure that also included a mosque, hospital, school and an asylum. It's tourist friendly – in fact few locals visit – and so it's a comfortable option for an introduction, a place where couples and families can go in together. All the soapers are male. It's best to make reservations.

Eminönü

If Sultanahmet is the Istanbul of postcards, Eminönü is the Istanbul of ferry schedules. It's the departure point for ferries up the Bosphorus, across to Asia and out to the Princes' and Marmara Islands. A few services also head up the Golden Horn, an inlet of the Marmara some 7.5 kilometres (five miles) long. The maritime traffic here is frantic, as hulking vessels skirmish with tiny motorboats for berthing positions. Pedestrian traffic is intense too – watch your wallet.

The commercial hub of the old city and a port since Ancient Greek times, its bustling waterfront leads back to a maze of alleys, mosques and the **Egyptian Bazaar**.

The Orient Express last rolled into **Sirkeci Station** back in 1961, and the former elegance of the area can still just be discerned under a layer of dust. The most characteristic, and interesting, aspect of the area, though, is the hubbub of the waterfront. Watching the ferries, tankers, fishing boats and cruise liners criss-cross the Golden Horn from a vantage point on **Galata Bridge** – a two-tier bridge with cafés and restaurants along its lower deck – is a fascinating way to while away an hour.

Sights & museums

Egyptian Bazaar

Mısır Çarşısı

Yeni Camii Meydanı (0212 513 6597). Tram Eminönü. **Open** 8am-7pm Mon-Sat. **Map** p50 C1/2 56

In front of the New Mosque is a pigeon-plagued plaza busy with itinerant street sellers and dominated on its south side by the high brick arch leading into the Egyptian Bazaar, also known as the Spice Bazaar. The market was constructed as part of the mosque complex, and its revenues helped support philanthropic institutions. The name derives from its past association with the arrival of the annual 'Cairo caravan', a flotilla of ships bearing rice, coffee and incense from Egypt.

While the bazaar's L-shaped vaulted hall is undeniably pretty, at first glance its 90 shops seem to be hustling nothing more than an assortment of oily perfumes, cheap gold and sachets of 'Turkish Viagra'. It's a tourist trap, to be sure, but to dismiss it out of hand is to miss one of the world's finest delis: make a beeline for Erzincanlılar (shop no.2) for delicious honeycomb and the mature hard Turkish cheese known as *eski kaşar*. Other food shops worth checking out are Pinar (no.14) for excellent *lokum* (Turkish delight); Antep Pazarı (no.50) for pistachios, nuts, honey-covered mulberries and dried figs stuffed with walnuts; and Güllüoğlu Baklavacısı (no.88) for pastries. Özel (no.82) has pretty, cheap scarves. Another reason to visit the market is to lunch at Pandeli's, a Greek-run restaurant up a flight of steps just inside the main entrance.

Running west from the market, Hasırcılar Caddesi is one of the city's most vibrant and aromatic streets thanks to a clutch of delis, including Namlı Pastırmacı, spice merchants and coffee sellers. Among them is Kurukahveci Mehmet Efendi, where caffeine addicts queue at the serving hatch to purchase the own-brand bags of beans.

Further along the street, look out for the arched doorways where flights of stairs lead up to the Rüstem Paşa Mosque, built in 1561 for a grand vizier of Süleyman the Great.

Galata Bridge
Tram Eminönü. **Map** p50 C1/p51D1 ⑰
The best place to observe the hustle and bustle is from the Galata Bridge, the vital link between the two sides of European Istanbul. The current structure, an unsightly concrete ramp with four steel towers at its centre, replaces a much-loved earlier bridge. This one was built in the 1980s to accommodate growing traffic. The lower deck of restaurants, bars and tea houses right on the waterfront provides ring-side seating for cheap beers and boat-watching. It's probably best not to eat along here (or if you do, keep a close eye on the bill); head instead to the fresh fish stalls at the west side of either end of the bridge.

New Mosque
Yeni Camii
Eminönü Meydanı (0212 527 8505).
Tram Eminönü. **Open** 7am-dusk daily.
Admission free. **Map** p50 C1 ⑱
Construction on the mosque began in 1598, but suffered a setback when the architect was executed for heresy. It was eventually completed in 1663, after the classical period of Ottoman architecture had passed. It is nonetheless a regal structure, particularly uplifting when seen floodlit. The fact that it is so obviously a working mosque tends to keep visitors at bay, but nobody objects to non-Muslims entering.

Rüstem Paşa Mosque
Rüstem Paşa Camii
Hasırcılar Caddesi 90 (0212 526 7350).
Tram Eminönü. **Open** 9am-dusk daily.
Admission free. **Map** p50 C1 ⑲
Above the shops, (whose rents pay for its upkeep), the mosque is invisible from the street. It's quite a city secret, although it's one of the most beautiful mosques built by Sinan. Smaller than most of his works, it's also set apart by its liberal and dazzling use of coloured tiles. The first-floor forecourt, with its colonnaded canopy and potted plants high above the crowded alleys, is one of Istanbul's loveliest hideaways.

Eating & drinking

Two blocks south of Sirkeci Station, narrow **Ibni Kemal Caddesi** is a street full of cheap eateries serving the local working population. The presence of neighbouring Hoca Paşa Mosque means no alcohol is served, but a meal costs less than YTL15 per person. The underslung section of the **Galata Bridge** is

Egyptian Bazaar p71

Galata Bridge p72

also crammed with budget fish restaurants, Sat, with menus in English and beer by the flagon. Much better, however, are the floating fish stalls on the west side of the bridge. Order an anchovy sandwich and watch the fishermen.

Hamdi Et Lokantası

Kalçın Sokak 17, Tahmis Caddesi (0212 528 0390). Tram Eminönü. **Open** 11am-midnight daily. **$**. **Turkish**. Map p50 C1 ⑥⓪

Right on Eminönü square, Hamdi is a favourite among Istanbul natives, particularly business lunchers and carniverous fans of south-eastern Turkish food. Hamdi serves meat *alaturca* at its very best, grilled to succulent perfection on the *mangal*. The restaurant occupies four floors, but the top one is the most memorable. In an enclosed glass terrace, it offers sweeping views of the Golden Horn and Beyoğlu. It's particularly lovely in the summer, when the windows are opened. Otherwise, opt for the curious Oriental Saloon on the first floor, kitted out with cuckoo clocks and startled nymphs.

North Shield

Ebusuud Caddesi 2 (0212 527 0931, www.thenorthshield.com). Tram Gulhane. **Open** noon-1am Mon-Thur, Sun; noon-4am Fri, Sat. **Pub**. Map p51 D3 ⑥①

The North Shield transports its regulars to sub-urban middle England. Think tartan carpets, Famous Grouse mirrors, etched glass screens, wooden benches and a dark, polished bar. There's even Abba, Elton John and Santana on the sound system. Homesick Brits get together here and at five other North Shields locations around town. It's big on sports, especially football and rugby.

Orient Express Restaurant

Sirkeci Station, Istasyon Caddesi (0212 522 2280, www.orientexpress restaurant.net). Tram Sirkeci. **Open** 11.30am-midnight daily. **$$**. **Turkish**. Map p51 D2 ⑥②

An essential stop for fans of the Orient Express and Agatha Christie, this time warp is bang in the centre of Sirkeci station, the final stop of the world's most famous train. In warmer weather, tables are set outside on the station platform. The only obvious change in the dining room since the restaurant's launch in 1890 is the incongruous concrete fishpond in the centre, which jars with the Oriental backdrop. The walls are adorned with black and white stills from the 1974 movie *Murder on the Orient Express*. Food is standard Turkish fare, reasonably priced. It's a shame the restaurant is usually empty.

Pandeli

Mısır Çarşısı 1, Eminönü Square (0212 527 3909, www.pandeli.com.tr). Tram Eminönü. **Open** 11.30am-7.30pm daily. **$$**. **Turkish**. Map p50 C1 ⑥③

Not a bad place for lunch if you're shopping in the Egyptian Bazaar. Occupying a wonderful set of domed rooms above the bazaar entrance, Pandeli is very much the essence of genteel old Stamboul. Decorated throughout in blue and white Iznik tiling, it's worth a visit for the interior alone. The food, by contrast, is run-of-the-mill Turkish and pricey and waiters have a tendency towards brusqueness. Ask for a table in the front room with views of the Golden Horn. Note the early closing time.

Shopping

Kalmaz Baharat

Mısır Çarşısı 41/1, Egyptian Bazaar (0212 522 6604). Tram Eminönü. **Open** 8am-7pm Mon-Sat. No credit cards. Map p50 C2 ⑥④

One of the oldest stores in the Egyptian Bazaar, this atmospheric place – just east of the main intersection – still has its original drawers and tea caddies. Specialities include spices, medicinal herbs, healing teas and aromatic oils.

Tunnel treasure

Archaelogical finds from the Marmaray Tunnel site.

The Marmaray Tunnel is the deepest rail tunnel in the world. When the project of which it is a part is completed, it will carry passengers and freight from Istanbul's European shore, south of the Golden Horn, to Üsküdar on the Asian shore. It is desperately needed to alleviate the city's chronic traffic problems. However, work has been plagued by setbacks and is currently three years behind schedule.

Digging under what has been the crossroads for great civilisations for centuries has its own unique challenges. In 2005, engineers found the remains of Portus Theodosiacus, a fourth-century Byzantine port, on the proposed site of the European terminal. More than 30 shipwrecks have been unearthed, including the only Byzantine galley ever found – one of the most important archaeological discoveries of recent times. There's also evidence of a settlement dating back to 6,000 BC, with skeletons and pottery discovered. In fact, so many artefacts have been uncovered that the Istanbul **Archaeology Museum** (see p53) has opened an exhibition dedicated to finds from the site.

It's a hard balancing act for the city. Every minute of delay costs $500, infrastructure can't hold up much longer, and yet heritage is irreplaceable.

Kurukahveci Mehmet Efendi

Tahmis Sokak 66 (0212 511 4262, www.mehmetefendi.com). Tram Eminönü. **Open** 8.30am-7pm Mon-Fri; 9am-6.30pm Sat. No credit cards. **Map** p50 C1 ⑥⑤

Reputedly the first shop to sell bagged Turkish coffee, Mehmet Efendi has been doing a roaring trade since 1871. It's located opposite the west entrance to the Egyptian Market – to find it, you'll just need to follow your nose. Besides the traditional Turkish variety, there's filter and espresso coffee, whole roasted beans, cocoa and *sahlep*, a winter drink made from ground orchid root.

Namlı Pastırmacı

Hasırcılar Caddesi 14-16 (0212 511 6393, www.namlipastirma.com.tr). Tram Eminönü. **Open** 8.30am-8pm Mon-Sat. **Map** p50 C1 ⑥⑥

A hugely popular deli just along from the west end of the Egyptian Market. It specialises in *pastırma* (Turkish pastrami) but also has a tantalising selection of cold cuts, cheeses, halva, honeycomb, *pekmez* (fruit-based molasses), olives and pickles.

Özgül Çeyiz

Mısır Çarşısı 83 (0212 522 7068, www.begonville.com.tr). Tram Eminönü. **Open** 8am-7.30pm Mon-Sat. **Map** p50 C1 ⑥⑦

The east end of the Egyptian Bazaar was once crammed with stores in the trousseau (*çeyiz*) business. In days of yore, young ladies were wheeled along by their female relatives to make wholesale purchases that would improve their prospects.

Özgül is one of the few survivors from those days. It's a minimal store packed with fancy embroidered sheets, quilts, towels and robes. Whether you're trousseau-hunting or not, there's some great stuff – such as the fluffy Begonville towels – at very reasonable prices.

Rüstem Paşa Mosque p72

Istiklal Caddesi p94

Beyoğlu

Beyoğlu is new Istanbul. The Istanbul of bars and restaurants, boutiques and artists' ateliers. The area's central artery is the ever-busy **Istiklal Caddesi**, where the entire city goes to work, shop and play, making it one of the liveliest streets on earth. Historically, the district went by two different names: **Galata**, for the hillside just north of the Golden Horn, and **Pera**, denoting what's now the lower Istiklal Caddesi area. Neighbourhoods such as **Çukurcuma** and **Cihangir** are among the city's mo st interesting: the former for antique shops and boutique hotels, the latter for stylish cafés. And after a day wandering their steep, narrow streets, head to buzzing **Nevizade Sokak** for dinner.

Beyoğlu is an area with boundaries that are hard to define, but for our purposes it includes everything up the hill from the Golden Horn, heading all the way north to **Taksim Square**.

Galata & Tünel

Echoing its mercantile origins, Galata remains almost completely commercial. Central to the area's history, and easily the most distinctive landmark north of the Golden Horn, the conical-capped **Galata Tower** has spectacular views from its pinnacle.

Opened in 1876, the one-stop funicular that runs from Karaköy up to **Tünel Square** at the southern end of Istiklal Caddesi is, after London and New York's systems, the third-oldest passenger underground in the world.

Tünel, the area around the upper station, is currently in transition from shabby neglect to arty affluence, with a proliferation of stylish cafés and restaurants.

Sights & museums

Arap Mosque
Arap Camii
*Galata Mahkemesi Sokak, Tersane
Caddesi.* **Open** 9am to dusk daily.
Admission free. **Map** p80 B4 ❶
Built between 1323 and 1337, and dedicated to St Dominic and St Paul, this
was the largest of Constantinople's
Latin churches. In the early 16th century, it was converted into a mosque
to serve the Moorish exiles from
Spain, which is possibly how it got its
current name, the 'Arab mosque'.
Despite extensive alterations, the
design is clearly that of a typical
medieval church, complete with apses
and a belfry.

Galata Mevlevihanesi
*Galip Dede Caddesi 15 (0212 245
4141).* **Open** 9.30am-4.30pm Mon,
Wed-Sun. **Admission** YTL2.
Map p80 C3 ❷
This is the only institution in Istanbul
dedicated to the Whirling Dervishes
that is open to the public. A peaceful
courtyard leads through to the octag-
onal *tekke* (lodge), a restored version
of the 1491 original, which contains
musical instruments and beautifully
illuminated Qu'rans. Also within the
complex is the tomb of Galip Dede, a
17th-century Sufi poet after whom the
street is named.

Galata Tower
Galata Kulesi
*Galata Square (0212 293 8180,
www.galatatower.net).* **Open** 9am-8pm
daily. **Admission** YTL10. No credit
cards. **Map** p80 C4 ❸
Originally named the Tower of Christ,
this watchtower was built in 1348 at
the apex of fortified walls. After the
Ottoman conquest, the tower was used
to house prisoners of war and later still
it became an observatory; during the
19th century, it was a look-out post to
watch for the fires that frequently
broke out in the city's largely wooden

buildings. In the 1960s, the tower
was restored and a horribly cheesy
restaurant and nightclub were added.
The restaurant, which remains, has
improved to some degree. However,
it's worth paying the rather hefty
entrance fee to ascend to the 360-
degree viewing gallery, which has
commanding views over the entire
sprawling metropolis.

Eating & drinking

Filled with an interesting mix
of restaurants, cafés and bars
frequented by locals, the narrow,
atmospheric streets stretching
from Tünel Square down to the
Galata Tower form a trendy but
low-key area, home to some of
the city's most exciting and
distinctive venues. Residents
come from all over the city to
catch Turkish musicians at
Badehane or jazz and pop
bands at **Babylon** (see p88).

Badehane
*General Yazgan Sokak 5 (0212 249
0550).* **Open** 9am-3am daily. **Bar**.
Map p80 C2 ❹
A modest, single-room venue just off
Tünel Square, Badehane began as an
eaterie, but quickly evolved into one of
the most popular bars in town. On
Wednesdays, live gypsy music (including local legend Selim Sesler) gets the
crowd dancing around the tiny, packed
tables. There is also live music on
Tuesdays and at weekends – see in-
house posters for details. In summer,
the café spills out on to the street,
where backgammon tournaments take
place, and friends meet for large beers
and a smoke.

Canim Ciğerim
*Asmalımescit Mahellesi, Minare Sokak
1 (0212 252 6060, www.asmalicanim
cigerim.com).* **Open** noon-midnight
daily. $$. No credit cards. **Turkish**.
Map p80 C2/p82 A5 ❺

ISTANBUL BY AREA

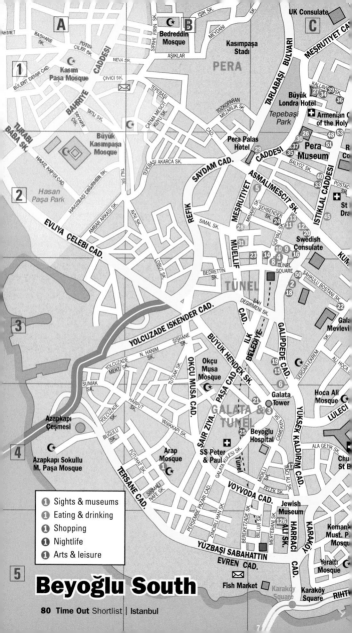

A   B   UK Consulate   C

Işık Sk.   ★ Bedreddin Mosque

Sıpahi Fırın Sk.   Meydanı   Kasımpaşa Stadı

MEŞRUTIYET CA

1   Kasım Paşa Mosque   PERA

CADDESİ   BAHRİYE   Çivici Sk.   Büyük Londra Hotel   KALLAVİ 49 Sk.   34

TURABİ BABA SK.   TATLI SK.   Çatma Mescit Kutlu Sk.   CAD.   Tepebaşı Park   Armenian C of the Holy

Büyük Kasımpaşa Mosque   TEPEBAŞI AKARCA SK.   CADDESİ   Pera Palas Hotel   25   26   27   35   37   Pera Museum   48   53   51   R   Co

2   Hasan Paşa Park   SAYDAM CAD.   REFİK   MEŞRUTİYET   ASMALIMESCİT SK.   BALYOZ SK.   40   33   İSTİKLAL CADDESİ   POSTAC

EVLİYA ÇELEBİ CAD.   SIMAL SK.   MİNARE SK.   ŞEHBENDER SK.   24   13   11   45   St I Dra

28   MUELLİF   31   23   5   10   4   8   9   12   16   Swedish Consulate   KUM

TÜNEL SQUARE   50   ŞAH   2   18   ŞAHKULU BOSTANI SK.   22

BEDRETTİN SK.   TÜNEL   DEĞİRMEN SK.   Gala Mevlevi

3   YOLCUZADE İSKENDER CAD.   N. HANIM SK.   SİŞHANE SK.   BÜYÜK HENDEK SK.   İLK BELEDİYE CAD.   GALİPDEDE CAD.   SERDAREKREM SK.   ALİ HOCA S

YOLCUZADE MEKT. SK.   Okçu Musa Mosque   PAŞA CAD.   19   15   Galata Tower   Hoca Ali Mosque

SUMAK SK.   HARPUT SK.   OKÇU MUSA CAD.   ŞAİR ZİYA.   21   GALATA & TÜNEL   3   YÜKSEK KALDIRIM CAD.   LÜLECİ

Azapkapı Çeşmesi   YOLCUZADE   BUĞULU SK.   YANIKKAPI SK.   25   Beyoğlu Hospital   ALA GEYİK SK.   Chu St B

4   Azapkapı Sokullu M. Paşa Mosque   Arap Mosque   FUTUHAT SK.   SS Peter & Paul   GALATA KULESİ SK.   MEŞRULİ   FELEK SK.   17

TERSANE CAD.   SIRMALI NAFE SK.   VOYVODA CAD.   Jewish Museum   126   Kemank Must. P Mosqu

① Sights & museums   PERŞEMBE PAZARI CAD.   ZİNCİRLİ HAN SK.   BİLLUR SK.   MERTEBANI SK.   HARRACI ALİ SK.   KARAKÖ

① Eating & drinking   YUZBAŞI SABAHATTİN   Yeraltı Mosque

① Shopping   EVREN CAD.   Fish Market   Karaköy   Karaköy Square   RIHT

① Nightlife

① Arts & leisure

Beyoğlu South

80 Time Out Shortlist | Istanbul

Beyoğlu North

1 Sights & museums
1 Eating & drinking
1 Shopping
1 Nightlife
1 Arts & leisure

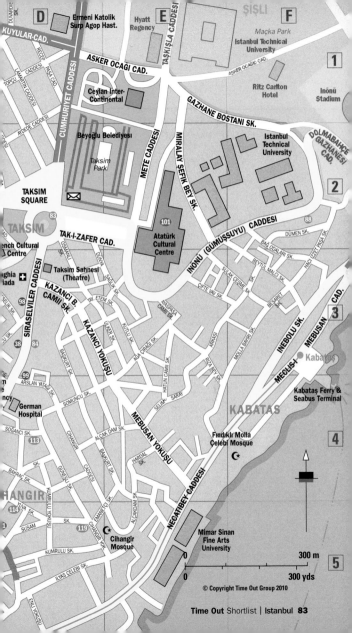

Home comforts

The House Café group goes from strength to strength.

The careful mixing of several key ingredients is needed to make a good café: happy staff, good food, a relaxed atmosphere and a sensitively designed space. A good café is a place to linger over coffee, enjoy a quick snack with friends or tap away on a laptop all afternoon. Branches of the House Café, a small chain of 11 venues, are good cafés.

The most striking aspect of each of the House Cafés is the design. The firm behind the fabulous interiors is Autoban, an Istanbul agency that won the *Wallpaper** Best Young Designer Award in 2004. Mixing retro styles, modern touches and elements of 19th-century Ottoman opulence, each of the cafés acknowledges and preserves the character of its host building (an Ottoman mansion, a

waterfront *yalı*, a new shopping mall). Almost every element of the interiors, from the lighting to the tables, is designed by Autoban.

'The House Café let us do what we wanted. It's the project we are most proud of,' explains Seyhan Özdemir, one of Autoban's joint founders. 'We can experiment with new designs in the House Cafés.'

House Café began as an open-house café for a group of friends. It was so popular that the owners realised there was a niche in the market, and the first House Café was opened in 2002 in an old Nişantaşı apartment. 'We wanted a cosy environment with delicious food and great service,' assistant general manager Erensah Ayanlar says. 'It was a new concept in Istanbul; there were only traditional Turkish tea houses before.'

The food policy was also a departure from the Turkish norm. Using seasonal ingredients, executive chef Coskun Uysal (previously of Jamie Oliver's Fifteen and the River Café) has created a diverse and interesting menu, with dishes suitable for different times of the day.

House Café's expansion has been impressive. Today, there are ten locations in Istanbul and one in Ankara. Each is successful and busy. 'The House Café is a lifestyle,' Erensah says.

Now, with Autoban's design input, the House Café is moving into hotels. The first House Hotel (see p145) has opened in Çukurcuma, and another is planned above the lovely House Café in Ortaköy (see p129).

There are only three choices at this perennially popular neighbourhood restaurant: beef, chicken or lamb. Once the meat of choice is ordered, a plate of mint, a plate of parsley, some spicy tomato sauce, a pile of flat bread and grilled veg will be plonked down, followed by around nine skewers of meat. It isn't licensed. Eat inside or on the terrace.

Enginar

Şah Kapısı Sokak 4A (0212 251 7321). **Open** noon-2am daily. **Bar**. **Map** p80 C4 ⑥

The neighbourhood around the Galata Tower has had a major facelift in the last few years: streets have been repaved and cafés have spread their tables across the spruced-up square surrounding the tower. Enginar, one of the area's most popular bars, has a claim to fame as a set for a local soap opera, and with its stained-glass windows and rustic interior, it is a perfect pit-stop after a tour of the tower or midway on the steep climb from Karaköy to Tünel. There's occasional music during the winter months.

Iskele Balik

Galata Bridge (no phone). **Open** 7am-midnight daily. **$**. No credit cards. **Seafood**. **Map** p80 C5 ⑦

There are dozens of restaurants around the fish market by Galata Bridge and on the bridge itself. This one, on the west side of the bridge, is consistently the most popular with locals. Take a seat on the patio out back, under a makeshift roof, and order the anchovies. A large plate of fried fish, two big hunks of soft bread and a small salad will arrive, priced YTL6.

KV Café

Tünel Geçidi 10 (0212 251 4338, www. kv.com.tr). **Open** 8am-2am daily. **Café (licensed)**. **Map** p80 C3 ⑧

Opposite Tünel station, an elaborate iron gate leads to an enchanting 19th-century arcade overgrown with potted plants. Of the handful of cafés lucky enough to share this secret passageway, KV is the largest and most atmospheric. Couples cosy up on wrought-iron furniture, snacking on cakes or lingering over cheese and wine. Inside, the café occupies three beautiful bare-brick rooms with tiled floors, arched windows, and unusual antiques. At dusk, the setting is even more romantic, lit by candles and Victorian lamps, with live piano music wafting through the arcade. The music programme is usually from September to March.

Lokal

Müeyyet Sokak 5/A, off Istiklal Caddesi (0212 245 5744). **Open** 10am-midnight daily. **$$**. **European/International**. **Map** p80 C2 ⑨

Once one of the hippest eateries in town, Lokal has graduated to classic status. On a tiny side-street off Asmalımescit, Lokal is easy to locate thanks to the films projected on the wall opposite, ranging from footage of skateboarders to spaghetti westerns. Menus bound by kitsch LP covers read like an encyclopedia of global fusion: pesto linguine, chicken tikka, pad Thai, salmon teriyaki and chicken wings. All are surprisingly good. There are two recent Lokal additions in the side streets around the original. One focuses on Italian food, while the one opposite Tünel offers coffee, smoothies and snacks.

Otto Sofyalı

Sofyalı Sokak 22/A (0212 252 6588, www.ottoistanbul.com). **Open** 11am-2am Mon-Sat. **Café/bar**. **Map** p80 C2 ⑩

With their authentic pizzas, light bites and good cocktails, Otto has been an important part of Istanbul food and drink as well as nightlife since the first branch opened back in 2005 (at the Santralistanbul arts centre). This branch has a similar industrial chic look to the others. Its most noticeable detail is the bar, which spans from the entrance all the way down to the back of the narrow venue.

Other locations Otto Beyoğlu, Asmalımescit Mahallesi, Şehbender Sokak 5/1, Tünel (0212 292 7015).

Refik

Sofyalı Sokak 10-12 (0212 243 2834). **Open** noon-3pm, 7-11.30pm Mon-Fri; 7pm-midnight Sat. **$$. Turkish.** **Map** p80 C2/p82 A5 ⓫

Established in 1954, this upmarket *meyhane* is a great starting point to immerse yourself in meze culture and acquire a taste for *rakı*. Gravel-voiced Refik Arslan still meets patrons at the door, including a devoted clientele of leftie hacks and intellectuals. Most regulars smoke and drink more than they eat, but the place is renowned for seafood dishes from the Black Sea. There's no music, as it would interfere with the animated conversation.

Şimdi

Asmalımescit Sokak 5 (0212 252 5443). **Open** 8am-2am daily. **Café/bar.** **Map** p80 C2/p82 A5 ⓬

This relaxed refuge off Istiklal is one of the most stylish all-day café-bars anywhere in Istanbul. Hipsters hang out in the retro front room, where low seating and low lighting encourage lounging. And with free wireless internet, you can bring your own laptop or use the Mac provided. There's an above-average selection of wine by the glass, accompanied by addictive balls of spiced cheese. Simple but delicious Mediterranean dishes are served in the dining area at the rear.

Sofyalı 9

Sofyalı Sokak 9 (0212 245 0362, www.sofyali.com.tr/eng). **Open** noon-1am Mon-Sat. **$. Turkish. Map** p80 C2/p82 C5 ⓭

A *meyhane* maybe, but *très* genteel. This cosy local haunt feels like someone's front room – someone with money, taste and a fine old house. The

ground floor space is smal – with mustard walls, exposed brickwork, wooden floors and hanging lanterns. But tables spill into the alley and there are two floors upstairs. Even so, reservations are a must, as the city's literati and gay crowd love this place. The food is a cut above – superior meze, followed by meat and fish dishes prepared with the freshest ingredients and a lightness of touch.

Shopping

Artrium

Tünel Gecidi İş Hanı, A Blok 3, 5, & 7 (0212 251 4302). **Open** 9am-7pm Mon-Sat. **Map** p80 C2 ⓮

A shop attracting a more sophisticated breed of collector, with three spacious display rooms and a prime location in the passage just across from KV Café. It has a fine selection of miniatures, maps, prints and calligraphy, along with Kütahya ceramics and the odd film and advertising poster.

Binbavul

Galipdede Caddesi 66 (0212 243 7218, binbavul@gmail.com). **Open** 11am-9pm Sun-Thur; 11am-11pm Fri-Sat. **Map** p80 C3 ⓯

Binbavul is located in the basement of an old building along an alley off the touristy Galip Dede Caddesi. The small street stall only hints at the cavernous space behind, which is rammed with vintage clothes, military regalia, theatre props, luggage, ball dresses, vinyl, designer goods and any whimsical item the owner picks up.

Erkul Cosmetics

Istiklal Caddesi 311 (0212 251 7662). **Open** 10.30am-10pm Mon-Sat; noon-10pm Sun. **Map** p80 C3 ⓰

A one-stop cosmetics store where you can find every grooming product imaginable. In addition to its own range, Erkul stocks reasonably priced perfumes and cosmetics from around the world.

Badehane p79

Grape expectations

Turkey's wine hits the international stage.

Wine isn't the first thing that comes to mind when thinking about Turkish products. Turkish delight, evil eye ornaments... But wine? That may be about to change. After touring Turkish vineyards in 2010, Master of Wine Tim Atkin commented: 'This historic, but little-known wine-producing country has an exciting range of indigenous varieties that deserve to reach a wider audience.'

The critics at the 2010 London International Wine Fair agreed, with Turkish wines scooping numerous medals and awards. But it's been a challenge to get the wineindustry up to competing standards when the anise-based spirit rakı is the traditional drink of choice, selling more than all other types of alcohol put together. In addition to a lack of demand at home, the industry has been hampered by the fact that three principal producers – Doluca, Kavaklidere and Kayra – have dominated the winemaking industry, tending to push small-scale vineyards to the sidelines. However, with international acknowledgement and increased exposure, Turkey is on the way to becoming a significant exporter.

'There's a long wine history in Turkey, but at the moment there's not much competition,' explained Murat Bozok, head chef of leading Istanbul restaurant Mimolett. 'When there is, the quality of wine will go up. We have a lot of boutique vineyards and the baby boom generation are beginning to learn about wines.'

Educating consumers about Turkey wines is half the battle. Below is a brief guide.

Öküzgözü (okoo-zgoo-zu) The name means 'bull's eye', after the large, dark grape. Medium body, not too fruity, but with some black fruits.

Boğazkere (bo-aahz-kere) Dark and rich, but typically used to make light-bodied blends.

Emir Refreshing and dry white with lingering floral and faintly fruity notes.

Narince An aromatic white with a smooth texture.

■ If you'd like to learn more and sample some of Turkey's top wines, visit **La Cave** (see p114), **Mimolett** (see p103) or **Sensus** (see right).

Konak Patisserie

Bereket Zade Mahallesi, Hacı Ali Sokak (0212 252 5346). **Open** 7am-7pm daily; 7am-midnight terrace. **Map** p80 C4 🟡

This French-influenced patisserie has been serving its colourful cakes since 1975. Alongside the cakes are sweet Turkish bite-sized pastries. There is a great view from the terrace.

Lale Plak

Galipdede Caddesi 1 (0212 293 7739). **Open** 9am-7.30pm Mon-Sat; 11.30am-7pm Sun. **Map** p80 C3 🟡

In business for 45 years, the city's top jazz, ethnic and classical music retailer is a favourite hangout of visiting jazz musicians. There is also a comprehensive selection of traditional Turkish music. Staff are knowledgeable and helpful.

Librairie de Pera

Galipdede Caddesi 22 (0212 243 7447, www.librairiedepera.com). **Open** 9am-7pm daily. **Map** p80 C3 🟡

This shop carries old and rare books in numerous languages, many concerned with travel and Turkey.

Paşabahçe

Istiklal Caddesi 314 (0212 244 0544, www.pasabahce.com.tr). **Open** 10am-8pm Mon-Thur; 10am-8.30pm Fri, Sat; 11am-7pm Sun. **Map** p80 C2/p82 A5 🟡

This stylish shop on three floors, a favourite with Istanbul's upwardly mobile, is Turkey's answer to Habitat. Head to the basement for kitchenware, basic china and glass, the ground floor for vases and ornaments, and the first floor for special collections. The latter includes impressive hand-blown glass, using traditional motifs – a conscious revival of time-honoured techniques.

Sensus

🟦 NEW *Bereketzade Mahallesi, Büyükhendek Caddesi 5 (0212 245 5657, www.sensuswine.com).* **Open** 10am-10pm daily. **Map** p80 C4 🟡

There are more than 370 different types of wine available in this underground cellar by Galata Tower. A tasting bar allows customers to try 50 wines by the glass (a five-glass flight is YTL20-YTL25; and for only YTL7.50 this can be accompanied with regional cheese).

Simay Bülbül

Camekan Sokak 5 (0212 292 7899, www.sim-ay.com). **Open** 10am-7pm Mon-Fri; 11am-8pm Sat-Sun. **Map** p80 C3 🟡

Designer Simal Bülbül's eponymous store sells her delicate leather and fabric clothes. She elegantly integrates leather into dresses and blouses with the lightest of touches to create appealing garments. There are also shoes and leather accessories.

Ümit Ünal

Ensiz Sokak 1B (0212 245 7886, www.umitunal.com). **Open** 10am-7.30pm Mon-Fri; 10am-noon Sat. No credit cards. **Map** p80 C2 🟡

Ümit Ünal is an Istanbul-based designer who is plugged into the international fashion scene. His avant-garde fashion shows are more like performances, and his multi-layered, complex creations are art installations as much as garments. Ünal's influences are diverse – Celtic banshees, Himalayan mountain tribes, gypsies. He travels the globe in search of unusual fabrics and accessories.

Nightlife

Badehane (p79) is a popular spot for Turkish music. There's low-key jazz every evening in winter at **KV** (see p85).

Babylon

Şehbender Sokak 3 (0212 292 7368, www.babylon.com.tr/en). **Open** 9.30pm-2am Tue-Thur; 10pm-3am Fri, Sat. Closed mid July-mid Sept. **Map** p80 C2/p82 A5 🟡

Far and away Istanbul's finest live music venue, this modestly sized brick vault with a mezzanine hosts some of the best parties in town. There's a lot of jazz, but Babylon is also the place for world music, electronica and anything avant-garde, and consistently attracts the best local and international names. Club nights range from funk to Oldies But Goldies parties, where cheesy ballads and dirty dancing are *de rigueur*. Pick up the well-distributed monthly brochure for details. Also on the premises is the Babylon Lounge, which serves food and decent cocktails.

Nardis Jazz Club

Galata Kulesi Sokak 14 (0212 244 6327, www.nardisjazz.com). **Open** 8.30pm-2am Mon-Sat. **Map** p80 B4 ㉕
Nardis is a dedicated jazz venue, just a few steps downhill from the Galata Tower, for patrons who know their jazz. Small and sparsely decorated – bare floorboards and brick walls – Nardis benefits from an intimate atmosphere. The place is run by guitarist and regular performer Önder Focan and his wife, who also edit *Jazz* magazine. Food is served, if you want it. Reservations are essential for tables near the stage. The music usually kicks off around 9.30pm or 10pm.

Pera

It was during the 19th century that Pera acquired its present character. The increased use of iron and brick, instead of the traditional wood, made it feasible to construct buildings that could survive the fires that regularly ravaged the city.

After the foundation of the Republic in the 1930s, what is now thought of as Pera, and the area beyond, officially became known as Beyoğlu and blossomed with new restaurants, theatres and concert halls.

West of Istiklal Caddesi is the lively neighbourhood of Asmalımescit, home of the city's low-rent art scene. The back streets are full of studios and galleries, as well as countless laid-back cafés, bars, and cheap eateries.

Meşrutiyet Caddesi is the address of the swish Pera Museum, as well as the famed Pera Palas Hotel, with its Orient Express associations and celebrity-filled guest book.

Sights & museums

Pera Museum
Pera Müzesi

141 Meşrutiyet Caddesi (0212 334 9900, www.peramuzesi.org.tr). **Open** 10am-7pm Tue-Sat; noon-6pm Sun. **Admission** YTL7; free-YTL5 reductions. No credit cards. **Map** p80 C2/p82 A4 ㉖
In an 1893 building that formerly housed Istanbul's famous Bristol Hotel, this well-run museum combines permanent exhibitions, art galleries, an auditorium, shop and café. Exhibits range from the arcane – a collection of Anatolian weights and measures – to the decorative: Kütahya tiles and ceramics. There is a major collection of 17th- to 19th-century European Orientalist art. Also look out for work by Osman Hamdi, including his most famous painting, *The Tortoise Trainer*. The temporary exhibitions of big-name artists, such as Botero, are usually excellent.

Eating & drinking

Büyük Londra

Meşrutiyet Caddesi 53 (0212 293 1619). **Open** 4pm-2am daily. **Bar**. **Map** p80 C1/p82 A4 ㉗
Fans of colonial watering holes tend to head for the bar at the Pera Palas Hotel; that's because they don't know about the Büyük Londra. Another late 19th-century time warp, it may be a little

less grand than the Pera Palas, but it's way more eccentric. The two gilded salons are plushly carpeted and decked with giant chandeliers. The immaculate barman occasionally sallies forth from the tiny bar at the back to change the 78 on the wind-up gramophone. Otherwise, the soundtrack is provided by caged songbirds on the window sills. Open late and rarely crowded, Büyük Londra is an open secret that's good to know. Hemingway stayed here in 1922, sent by the *Toronto Daily Star* to cover the Turkish war of independence, and the bar is still favoured by artists, writers and film crews.

Lokanta

Meşrutiyet Caddesi 145-147 (0212 245 5810). **Open** noon-3pm, 6.30pm-2am Mon-Thur; noon-3pm, 6.30pm-5am Fri, Sat. Closed July-Oct. **$$**. **Turkish**. Map p80 B2/p82 A5 ㉘

Lokanta roughly translates into English as 'canteen', appropriate given the plain decorative style. No matter, it's all about the food, notable for top-quality ingredients and an unfussy approach. The atmosphere is low-key and casual, and the place is usually busy, with a constant hum of conversation – just like a *lokanta*. This is a very enjoyable place to spend time during winter weekends; in summer the same menu and staff move upstairs to their fashionable terrace venue, which has a panoramic view.

Mikla

The Marmara Pera, Meşrutiyet Caddesi 167-185 (0212 293 5656, www.miklarestaurant.com). **Open** 6.30pm-11.30am Mon-Sat. **$$$$**. **Modern European**. Map p80 C2/ p82 A4 ㉙

On the roof garden of the 18-storey Marmara Pera Hotel, Mikla is one Istanbul's most exclusive eateries. The project of Turco-Finnish chef Mehmet Gürs, the menu reflects both sides of his heritage and is brief but inventive. Starters are big enough to share (just

as well, as prices are steep). Mains might include grilled grouper with tomatoes, aubergines, anchovies, capers, olive oil and poached artichoke, or pistachio-crusted lamb chops with potato, pistachio purée and pomegranate molasses. The place doesn't fill up until 10.30pm, so don't book too early or you'll miss the buzz.

Nu Teras

Meşrutiyet Caddesi 67 (0212 245 6070, www.nupera.com.tr). **Open** June-Oct 6.30pm-2am Mon-Thur, Sun; 6.30pm-5am Fri, Sat. **Modern Turkish/Bar**. Map p82 C2/ p82 A4 ㉚

On the rooftop of the Nu Pera building, Nu Teras is the epitome of hip Istanbul – with the backdrop of a stunning view of the Golden Horn. The area behind the bar is given over to long tables for diners, who tuck into the same nouvelle Turkish cuisine as at Lokanta (see left), the winter venue on the ground floor. Dancing is tolerated, but swaying is considered cooler. This was the first Beyoğlu venue to lure posh Turks from their usual haunts in Etiler. Unlike other new venues that were crowded out then swiftly abandoned, Nu Teras is a survivor that can be considered a classic.

Public

NEW *Meşrutiyet Caddesi 84 (0212 251 5131)*. **Open** noon-midnight Mon-Thur; noon-4am Fri, Sat. **Mediterranean/ Bar**. Map p80 B2/p82 A5 ㉛

Public is a new Beyoğlu venture from the team at Happily Ever After, the upscale Bebek venue. Whereas Happily Ever After is preppy, Public's decor is urban chic – befitting its location among the new hotels and design bars of Meşrutiyet. By day, it serves an impressive range of snacks and light lunches. The evening menu is more substantial, with Mediterranean dishes and a few Turkish standards. The music gets going at night too; some of Istanbul's more cutting-edge DJs and a few international names have put in an appearance. After dark, Public is all about the partying.

Rejans

Emir Nevrus Sokak 7A (0212 243 3882, www.rejansrestaurant.com). **Open** noon-3pm, 7pm-midnight Mon-Sat. **$$$. Russian. Map** p80 C1/p82 B4 ❸❷

Founded by White Russians who relocated to Istanbul in the wake of the Russian Revolution, Rejans was reputedly one of Atatürk's favourite restaurants. Left-wing Turkish intellectuals would come here to gripe over borscht and vodka. Since the red star was spurned in favour of the gold card, Rejans is now frequented by visiting Russians with deep pockets, who knock back flavoured vodkas as they gorge on 'tsar's zakuski'. If the Slavic food is so-so, Rejans still oozes charm, with its polished wood, high ceilings, musicians' gallery and a drunken doorman to hang customers' coats on hooks personalised with the names of long-dead regulars.

Shopping

Ada Müzike

Orhan Adli Apaydın Sokak 20, off Istiklal Caddesi (0212 251 3878). **Open** 9am-10pm Mon-Thur, Sun; 9am-11pm Fri, Sat. **Map** p80 C2/p82 A5 ❸❸

Owned by local record company Ada, this was Istanbul's first shop to specialise in Turkish rock and protest music. The setting is surprisingly smart, and there's a small café and Biletix ticket booth attached. There's also a decent range of foreign CDs, newspapers and magazines.

Ambar

Kallavi Sokak 6, off Istiklal Caddesi (0212 292 9272, www.nuhun ambari.com). **Open** 8am-8pm Mon-Fri; 9.30am-8pm Sat. **Map** p80 C1/p82 A4 ❸❹

One of the few places in Istanbul that sells fresh tofu. Other worthwhile buys include wholegrain bread, organic grains and pulses, hulled pumpkin and sunflower seeds and a range of organic fruit and veg.

Nightlife

Things also hot up at **Public** (see p91) once the dinner plates have been pushed away.

11:11

NEW *Tepebaşı Mahallesi, Meşrutiyet Caddesi 69 (0212 244 8834, www.1111.com.tr).* **Open** 6pm-4am Wed-Sat. **Map** p80 C2/p82 A4 ❸❺

Looking like a James Bond baddie's lair, 11:11 is a busy venue that's popular with a more mature crowd. The remarkable decor looks like the inside of an ice cube. There are several different areas, each playing a different genre of music. A lounge bar also serves Asian and fusion food alongside good cocktails.

Ehli Keyif

Kallavi Sokak 20, off Istiklal Caddesi (0212 251 1010). **Open** noon-2am Mon-Sat. **Map** p80 C1/p82 B4 ❸❻

Tucked away on its own little street off Istiklal, this classic little *meyhane* has decent food and, most weekend nights, an exhilarating atmosphere. It has one of the best reputations for *fasil*, which makes reservations essential. Dancing in the street is not uncommon. Highly recommended.

Nu Club

Meşrutiyet Caddesi 67 (0212 245 6070). **Open** 11pm-4am Fri, Sat. Closed June-Sept. **Map** p80 C2/p82 A4 ❸❼

The Nu Pera complex is known for great modern Turkish cuisine (at Lokanta) and amazing views (at Nu Teras). Come winter, the action moves downstairs to this intimate basement club, where everyone knows everyone, and anyone who doesn't soon

Nu Teras p91

will. Top-notch local DJs like Yunus Güvenen and Barış Türker are complemented with a guest DJ from Paris once a month. Unpretentious and great fun.

Tek Yön
Sıraselviler Caddesi 63/1 (0535 233 0654, www.tekyonclub.com). **Open** 10pm-4am daily. No credit cards. **Map** p83 D3 ⑧
Still one of the most happening gay venues in town, able to retain a few bears even as its new sound system, video screen and club tunes have begun packing in the clubbers, middle classes and foreigners. For a Turkish night on the tiles in an unthreatening environment, this is your best bet.

Xlarge
Caddesi Kallavi Sokak 12 (0506 788 7372). **Open** 11pm-5am Wed-Sat. No credit cards. **Map** p80 C1/p82 A4 ⑨
True to its name, this is a mega club. It features a ballroom-sized chandelier, the biggest bar of the venues here and two giant beds flanking the mezzanine bar. It's pretty busy, largely thanks to the recent DJ Mus-T programmes for avid dance music lovers. The Las Vegas-style drag revue brings Lady Gaga and Madonna to the stage. A pansexual crowd often roars in appreciation of the spectacle. **Other locations** Xlarge Chicos, Hüseyin Ağa Mahallesi, Küçük Bayram Sokak 1, off Istiklal Caddesi (0212 245 6898).

Istiklal Caddesi

Istiklal Caddesi gained its present name, 'Independence Street', soon after the founding of the Republic. In character, it remains resolutely pre-Republican, thanks to some wonderful early 20th-century architecture. The **Botter House** at nos.475-477 is an art nouveau masterpiece by Raimondo D'Aronco, built for Jean Botter,

Sultan Abdül-Hamit's tailor. A few doors up, at no.401, the **Mudo Pera** has an art nouveau interior of highly polished wood.

The street's churches are more restrained, often hidden from the street – the result of a restriction forbidding non-Muslim buildings from appearing on the skyline that held sway until the 19th century. The oldest is **St Mary Draperis** at no.429, a fairly humble building from 1789 that once served as the Austro-Hungarian embassy. This stretch of Istiklal is lined with former embassies, some still serving as consulates.

Hardly big enough to constitute a district, Galatasaray refers to the streets surrounding the **Galatasaray Lycée** (high school), founded in 1868. The current building, which dates from 1907, includes the small **Galatasaray Museum**, dedicated to Istanbul's top football team, which started life at the school. The slight widening of Istiklal in front of the Lycée is known as **Galatasaray Square**.

Sights & museums

Arter – Space for Art
Istiklal Caddesi 211 (0212 243 3767, www.arter.org.tr). **Open** 11am-7pm Tue-Thur; noon-8pm Fri-Sun. **Admission** free. **Map** p80 C2/ p82 A5 ⑩
See box right.

Eating & drinking

Discerning drinkers head to the stylish cafés and bars around the Galatasaray Lycée, where Istanbul's intellectuals, designers, and media types congregate. Photographers favour **Kafe Ara**, named after Magnum snapper Ara Güler, who lives upstairs.

360

NEW *Mısır Apartmani 32/309, Istiklal Caddesi (0212 251 1042, www.360 istanbul.com).* **Open** noon-4pm Mon-Fri; 6pm-2.30am Fri; 6pm-4am Sat; 6pm-2.30am Sun. **$$$**. **International**. Map p80 C1/p82 B4 ㊶

On the roof of the historic Mısır apartment block, 360 has magnificent 360-degree views of the city. The spacious dining area is a high-tech fusion of steel and glass with brick walls. The international menu includes dishes such as Thai green curry and slow-roast cherry duck, but the pizzas are a good bet. Reservations are essential on Fridays and Saturdays, with two sittings per night. It turns into a fairly boisterous club and cocktail after midnight, when the venue, and the view, are at their best.

Hacı Abdullah

Atfı Yılmaz Caddesi 9/A, off Istiklal Caddesi (0212 293 8561, www.haci abdullah.com.tr). **Open** 11am-10.30pm daily. **$**. **Turkish**. Map p82 C3 ㊷

One of the oldest restaurants in Istanbul, Hacı Abdullah is deservedly famous for traditional Ottoman fare. Three old-school dining rooms are brightened by a few contemporary flourishes. Opt for the pale pink room at the rear, complete with skylight and chandelier. The restaurant is renowned for its pickles, stored in colourful jars and bizarrely described in the English menu as 'the symbols of pooped politicians'. An array of pre-cooked dishes is on display in the front room. No alcohol is served.

Kafe Ara

Tosbağa Sokak 2, off Yeniçarşı Caddesi (0212 245 4105). **Open** 8am-midnight Mon-Thur, Sun; 10am-midnight Fri, Sat. **Café**. Map p80 C1/p82 B4 ㊸

A continental-style café owned by local Magnum photographer Ara Güler, whose evocative black and white shots of Istanbul adorn the

Blank canvas

Modern Turkish painting at the Arter Gallery.

The turret of the lifesize inflatable tank in the window deflates momentarily before standing to attention again. A group of teenagers outside in Istiklal Caddesi are enjoying the spectacle. It may not be the subtlest message, but its execution is flawless, and it's funny too. This was the centrepiece for the inaugural exhibition at **Arter – Space for Art** (see left), a new initiative from the Vehbi Koç Foundation set up to showcase cutting-edge Turkish art. It is the newest of a group of privately run and foundation-based galleries along Istiklal Caddesi.

The exhibition space was created to encourage and nurture Turkish contemporary art, especially multimedia work – an area that is only beginning to be explored fully in Turkey.

Across the gallery's five floors is a vast variety of often-controversial works in various media, including textiles, photography, sculpture, video installations and photomontage, from artists including Adel Abidin, Halil Altındere, Nevin Aladaş, Maja Bajeviç, Elina Brotherus and Cevdet Erek.

January 2011 will see the opening of Tactics of Invisibility – a collaborative exhibition with the Austrian-based Thyssen-Bornemisza Art Contemporary project.

walls and place mats. In fine weather, tables in the little alley opposite the Galatasaray Lycée fill up fast. In winter, the smart, split-level interior buzzes with cultured patrons armed with portfolios, notebooks, or laptops. No alcohol is served, but the fresh-pressed lemonade and milkshakes are great. Snack on sandwiches, pasta and desserts.

Kaktüs

Imam Adnan Sokak 4, off Istiklal Caddesi (0212 249 5979). **Open** 8am-2am daily. **Café/bar**. **Map** p82 C3 ㊹

Kaktüs's elegant dark-wood interior owes a great deal to the classic French café. Its patrons do their best to recreate the ambience of a Godard movie by chain-smoking and sipping blonde beers or black coffee. Stand-offish staff process the short-order menu, which changes daily. Since opening in the early 1990s, Kaktüs has spawned countless imitators, but it remains the coolest hang-out, with some of the highest prices. Cadde-i Kebir across the street is similar in style, but sells beer for about half the price.

Other locations 16 Cihangir Caddesi, Cihangir (0212 243 5731).

Leb-i Derya Richmond

Sixth Floor, Richmond Hotel, Istiklal Caddesi 445 (0212 243 4375, www.lebi derya.com). **Open** 11am-2am Mon-Thur, Sun; 11am-4am Fri, Sat. Closed lunch Jul, Aug. **$$$**. **Modern European/ Bar**. **Map** p80 C2/p82 A5 ㊺

Located on the sixth floor of the Richmond Hotel on Istiklal Caddesi, Leb-i Derya has probably the best views of any restaurant in the city, even by Istanbul standards. The tables are placed by vast windows: very romantic, especially if the meal is timed with the setting sun. Using the best ingredients, the dishes are simple but perfectly rendered. Highlights include parmesan-crusted sea bass, beef cheek ragu and scallop ravioli. And while the menu changes with the seasons, one constant is the extraordinary Forty-Spice Steak. The restaurant stops serving lunch in July and August due to the greenhouse effect of its glass panelling. Instead, go for sundowners, with breathtaking views of the Bosphorus and the Sea of Marmara. Reservations are recommended.

Other locations Kumbaracı Iş Hanı 57/7, Kumbaracı Yokuşu, Tünel (0212 293 4989).

Zoe

Tomtom Mahallesi, Yeniçarşı Caddesi 58/5 (0212 251 7491). **Open** noon-2am daily. **Bar/restaurant**. **Map** p81 D1/p82 B4 ㊻

Despite the gruff bouncers manning the red velvet entrance, Zoe is actually a relatively laid-back bar/restaurant that puts equal emphasis on food and drink. It's one of many venues that makes the most of its rooftop; in the summer, lively groups of customers party under the stars.

Shopping

Ali Muhiddin Hacı Bekir

Istiklal Caddesi 83/A (0212 244 2804, www.hacibekir.com.tr). **Open** 8am-10pm Mon-Sat; 9am-10pm Sun. **Map** p82 C3. ㊼

You can't come to Turkey without trying Turkish Delight. This place, which has been in the confection business since 1777, is where to try it and buy it. You should also suck on some *akide*, colourful boiled sweets that come in every conceivable flavour. Other tasty gifts include halva, baklava and marzipan (*badem ezmesi*), which all come in beautiful gift-wrapped boxes.

Denizler Kitapevi

Istiklal Caddesi 199/A (0212 243 3174, www.denizlerkitabevi.com). **Open** 10am-8pm daily. **Map** p80 C2/p82 A4 ㊽

The 130-year-old premises of Denizler Kitapevi once housed the Dutch

Consulate. This shop specialises in books on a maritime theme (*deniz* means 'sea'), but is also strong on travel guides, especially on Turkey.

Homer Kitapevi

Yeniçarşi Caddesi 12A (0212 249 5902). **Open** 10am-7.30pm Mon-Sat. **Map** p81 D1/p82 B4 ㊾

Alongside the Galatasaray Lycée, this smart, air-conditioned bookshop has what is widely considered to be the best collection of foreign non-fiction in the city. It's particularly strong on art and academic subjects.

Ipek

Istiklal Caddesi 230 (0212 249 8207). **Open** 9am-8pm Mon-Sat. **Map** p80 C3 ㊿

If it's neckwear you're after, this is the place to find it. Along with charming and persuasive service, you'll find an enormous range of scarves, shawls and ties in an exhaustive range of fabrics.

Mavi Jeans

Istiklal Caddesi 195 (0212 244 6255, www.mavi.com). **Open** 10am-10pm Mon-Sat; 11am-10pm Sun. **Map** p80 C2/p82 A4 (51)

Since making it big in the United States, Mavi's prices have rocketed, but compared with imported brands, they remain reasonable. The styles aren't particularly cutting edge, but the jeans are very wearable. T-shirts, sweatshirts and casual co-ordinates complete the look.

Mor

Turnacıbaşı Sokak 10B (0212 292 8817). **Open** 10am-7.30pm Mon-Sat. **Map** p81 D1/p82 C4 (52)

A stylish, glass-fronted studio just down from the Galatasaray Hammam, selling inspired originals designed by an in-house team. Most pieces are fashioned from silver and bronze, often combining scraps of ethnic jewellery from eastern Turkey, Turkmenistan and Afghanistan.

Robinson Crusoe

Istiklal Caddesi 195/A (0212 293 6968, www.rob389.com). **Open** 9am-9.30pm Mon-Sat; 10am-9.30pm Sun. **Map** p80 C1/p82 B4 (53)

A good-looking but cramped space saved by its tall ceilings, the book store has an especially well-chosen selection of English-language fiction, international music and art mags, plus an array of titles on Istanbul and Turkey.

Roll

Turnacıbaşı Sokak 11 (0212 244 9656). **Open** 10am-10pm Mon-Sat; noon-10pm Sun. **Map** p81 D1/p82 C4 (54)

Most vintage stock here is shipped from Europe and dates from the 1960s and '70s – loud nylon shirts, suede and velvet jackets, and vintage Adidas tracksuit tops.

Selim Mumcu Sahaf

Yeniçarşı Caddesi 33/C (0212 245 4496). **Open** 10am-8pm Mon-Sat. **Map** p81 D1/p82 B4 (55)

What the stock lacks in depth at this bookshop, it more than makes up for in eclecticism. There are also hundreds of old movie posters, photos, postcards and other memorabilia for sale.

Nightlife

Dirty

Erol Dernek Sokak 11/1, Hanif Han Apt (mobile 536 399 6151). **Open** 10pm-2am Wed-Sat. No credit cards. **Map** p81 D1/p82 C4 (56)

The underground venue of Dirty is known for its pop-art decor and constant stream of electronic DJs. Some frequent guest DJs include Mabbas, Style-Ist, Disc Jokey Ari, 7-Erhan.

Dogzstar

Tosboğa Sokkak 22 (0212 244 1081). **Open** 10.30am-10.30pm Mon-Thur, Sun; 2pm-4am Fri, Sat. **Map** p81 D1/p82 B4 (57)

It may be small, but Dogzstar proves that size doesn't matter: this little

Robinson Crusoe p97

club in Beyoğlu has garnered quite a reputation for itself: the laid-back, let-loose, neo-punk vibe here packs a punch. It can get a little cramped, but it's a good place to boogie, thanks to resident DJ Ari.

Eylül

Erol Dernek Sokak 16, off Istiklal Caddesi (0212 245 2415). **Open** noon-2am daily. **Map** p81 D1/p82 C4 ⑱

Eylül means September, but this folk-music bar engenders a kind of balmy, best-years-of-our-lives vibe all year round. A long-established venue with reliably good musicians and an all-singing, all-dancing crowd of up-for-it regulars, Eylül is a great place in which to while away the afternoons. The music kicks off around 3pm, so you don't have to eat. Evenings get much busier and tables are at more of a premium.

Indigo

Akarsu Sokak 1-5, off Istiklal Caddesi (0212 244 8567, www.livingindigo. com). **Open** 10pm-4am Tue-Thur, Sun; 11pm-5am Fri, Sat. **Map** p80 C1/p82 B4 ⑲

Attracting a mix of local and foreign bands and DJs, Indigo is the definitive venue for fans of electronic music. Smack in the centre of Beyoğlu, it is also jammed every weekend. So be warned: if you don't like people pushing you around, rubbing up against you and treading on your toes, it might be best to steer clear of the place. And as one of very few venues with an interest in new music, it has built up a loyal audience of electro-rockers who are prepared to queues for hours to get in, so it's best to arrive early or buy tickets in advance. In the summer, Indigo moves to its other venue, Blanco.

Studio Live

Atıf Yılmaz Caddesi 17/A (0212 244 7712, www.studiolive.com.tr). **Open** 10pm-4am Fri, Sat. **Map** p82 C3 ⑳

Along with Balans, Studio Live caters for both international acts and local cover bands, with the occasional DJ party thrown into the mix.

Arts & leisure

Emek

Yeşilçam Sokak 5, off Istiklal Caddesi (0212 293 8439). No credit cards. **Map** p82 C3 ⑱

During the golden age of Turkish cinema, Yeşilçam Sokak was Turkey's answer to Hollywood. No more. But the Emek still stands as a relic of former glories, built in the 1920s with an impressively ornate 875-seat hall. Forgive the newer lino flooring and sagging upholstery and catch a film here if you can.

Galatasaray Hamamı

Turnacıbaşı Sokak 24 (0212 252 4242 men, 0212 249 4342 women). **Open** *Men* 7am-10pm daily. *Women* 8.30am-8pm daily. **Map** p81 D1/p82 C4 ⑫

Built in 1481, for almost 500 years this hammam was for men only. A small women's section was finally added in 1963. Little else has been altered. The *camekan* is particularly fine, and there's some beautiful tilework at the entrance to the men's steam room. Unlike other hammams, the Galatasaray has marble slabs in the *soğukluk* where you can have a massage in semi-privacy. Because it's used largely by locals, the steam room is hot, hot, hot – towels have to be laid on the *göbektaşı* before anyone can lie on it. Staff are shameless about hustling for tips, but at least they give a good massage. To find the place, take the side-street off Istiklal Caddesi immediately north of the Galatasaray Lycée.

Garajistanbul

Tomtom Mahallesi, Yeni Çarşı Caddesi, Kaymakam Reşat Bey Sokak 11 (0212 212 4499, www.garajistanbul.org). **Map** p80 C1/p82 B4 ⑬

A forward-thinking performing arts centre, not afraid to lend its stage to any discipline, from cutting-edge theatre to the International Puppet Festival. The programme covers theatre, dance, music, literature and arts shows, both home-grown and from abroad. The non-profit organisation that runs the centre produces its own shows and tours and a magazine. The centre is also open to touring companies. There is a bar and café on the premises.

Taksim-Beyoğlu

Halep Pasajı, Istiklal Caddesi 140 (0212 251 3240, www.beyoglu sinemasi.com.tr). No credit cards. **Map** p82 B3 ⑥⑭

Directly across from the Atlas Pasajı, the Beyoğlu has an authentic art-house feel with a programme to match. From July to September, there's a daily programme of critics' picks from the past year, but this soon slides into anything from the past decade. Across from the foyer/café is the small-screen Pera, with the same management and similar screenings.

Yeşilçam

Imam Adnan Sokak 10, off Istiklal Caddesi (0212 293 6800, www.yesilcamsinemasi.com). No credit cards. **Map** p82 C3 ⑥⑮

At this small, basement art-house cinema, the programming leans towards local and European independent film. The charming foyer is full of old projection machines and fading film posters.

Nevizade

Beyoğlu nightlife once revolved around the *meyhanes* (Turkish tavernas) of **Çiçek Pasajı** (Flower Passage), an arcade facing the Galatasaray Lycée school gates. These days, it's almost exclusively frequented by tourists, a beautiful setting for an overpriced, mediocre meal. The adjacent Balık Pazarı

(**Fish Market**) is lined with shops fronted by wooden trays of piscine still-life on ice. Just beyond the fish market is **Nevizade Sokak**, the liveliest and loudest dining spot in Istanbul, crammed full of pavement restaurants.

On the east side of the fish market passage at no.24A, hidden behind big, black doors, is the **Armenian Church of the Three Altars** – it's rarely open, but take a look inside if you get the chance.

On the west side of Nevizade Sokak are two old arcades, the **Avrupa Pasajı** and **Aslıhan Pasajı**. The former is a mini Grand Bazaar, the latter is full of second-hand book and record shops.

Eating & drinking

A *meyhane* is where locals meet, eat meze, drink *rakı* and are cajoled by house musicians into belting out folk songs.

When ordering meze, the more dishes the merrier, since sharing is what it's all about. In Nevizade Sokak and around, cold dishes cost about YTL5, hot ones YTL6-YTL10, and seafood appetisers YTL10-YTL20. For two people, six dishes are usually enough. Most dishes can be chosen from the fridges, or will be paraded before you on a tray. Or go for a set menu of meze, fish, meat and dessert, with unlimited *rakı*, beer or wine, which costs about YTL40-YTL80 a head.

Boncuk

Nevizade Sokak 7A (0212 243 1219). **Open** 11.30am-2am daily. **Turkish**. **Map** p82 B3 ⑥⑥

This *meyhane* specialises in Armenian dishes and features live *fasıl* music.

Cumhuriyet Meyhanesi

Sahne Sokak 47, Balık Pazarı (0212 293 1977). **Open** 9.30am-2am daily. **Turkish**. **Map** p82 B3 ⑥⑦

Once frequented by Atatürk, this *meyhane* is notable for its *fasıl* musicians.

Gizli Bahçe

Nevizade Sokak 27 (0212 249 2192). **Open** noon-3am daily. **Bar**. Map p82 B3 ⑥⑧

The only way to tell this place apart from the dozens of other establishments on Nevizade Sokak is by the '27' crudely painted on the wall. There's a mellow bar on the ground floor and a livelier space up two flights of stairs, littered with low tables and armchairs. The name means 'Secret Garden' – and you'll find that upstairs, too. The music is an odd medley of modern electro and obscure 1980s tracks. The door policy can be uncharacteristically picky for the area.

James Joyce

Balo Sokak 26, off İstiklal Caddesi (0212 244 7970, www.theirish centre.com). **Open** noon-2am Mon-Thur, Sun; noon-4am Fri, Sat. **Pub**. Map p82 B3 ⑥⑨

The first and only Irish pub in Istanbul. The decor is predictably clichéd, although recently renovated, but the punters are a mixed bag of worldly Turks, expats and tourists who come for the decent range of fairly pricey beers (Guinness included). Irish breakfast is served all day and there's often live music. The place gets packed for international football matches, when the atmosphere can be electric. There's also regular live music on the new stage.

Krependeki Imroz

Nevizade Sokak 16 (0212 249 9073). **Open** 11.30am-2am daily. **Turkish**. Map p82 B3 ⑦⓪

Founded in 1941 and one of the oldest *meyhanes*, Krependeki Imroz deserves a mention for its excellent staff, solid food and reasonable price. Imroz is the Greek name for Gökçeada, one of the Aegean islands, and home to the Greek owners.

Mer Balik Restaurant

Hüseyin Ağa Mahallesi 23, Balık Pazarı (0212 292 8358, www.beyoglu mer.com). **Open** 11.30am-2am daily. **Turkish**. Map p82 B3 ⑦①

For quality fish (rather than a thrilling atmosphere), Mer Balik is better than most of the *meyhane* establishments around the area. The lantern fish kebab is outstanding.

Pano

Hamalbaşı Caddesi 12B (0212 292 6664). **Open** 11am-2am daily. **Wine bar**. Map p82 B3 ⑦②

Over a century old, Pano is an Istanbul institution. This atmospheric wine bar is like an updated take on a typical Greek taverna, with wood-panelled interior and rows of giant barrels above the bar. The later it gets, the more people pile in, and there's often standing room only. Then customers squeeze around the narrow counters, sampling Turkish and imported wines by the glass or bottle. Beer is also plentiful and cheap. Tasty finger food includes a generous cheese platter. Only the lucky few will find a table for a proper meze dinner.

Şahika

Nevizade Sokak 17 (0212 249 6196). **Open** noon-4am daily. **Bar/restaurant**. Map p82 B3 ⑦③

Another lively but laidback venue with dozens of stools and tiny tables packed into the small space outside, from where a predominantly younger crowd watches the world go by. Inside, wooden stairs lead to five levels of dining rooms and a summer roof terrace where the good times roll to a mix of 1980s, electronica and alternative rock. The simple menu is good value for money.

Shopping

Bünsa

Dudu Odaları Sokak 26, Balık Pazarı (0212 243 6265). **Open** 9am-8pm Mon-Sat. Map p82 B3 ⑦④

Herbal remedies and healing tonics, from medicinal teas to ginseng, karakovan honey and rare varieties of *pekmez* (fruit molasses). Tell them your ailment, and they'll prescribe a potion. The most popular panacea is a concoction of honey, royal jelly, nettle and ginseng, guaranteed to beat fatigue.

Mimplak

Aslıhan Sahaflar Çarşısı 49 (0212 252 6877). **Open** noon-8pm daily. **Map** p82 B3 **75**

In a passageway crammed with second-hand book and record shops, this tiny shop is the best of the lot. Look for bargain deals on old disco and soundtrack albums, plus rare Turkish releases.

Seyitağaoğulları Carpet Kilim Hand Crafts

Avrupa Pasajı 15 (off Balık Pazarı), Meşrutiyet Caddesi 16 (0212 249 2903). **Open** 9.30am-8.30pm daily. **Map** p82 B3 **76**

Kilim accessories are everywhere these days, but what you'll find here – from belts and footwear to bags, purses and stationery – is a cut above the rest. The products are all handmade, the kilims are kosher and the leather trim really is leather.

Şütte

Dudu Odaları Sokak 21, Balık Pazarı (0212 293 9292). **Open** 9am-8pm Mon-Sat. **Map** p82 B3 **77**

This long-established deli, owned by Macedonians, is one of the few places in Istanbul that stocks pork products other than bacon. It also carries pricey but wonderful imported cheeses, plus cheaper local cheeses, ready-made meze and condiments.

Nightlife

Balans

Balo Sokak 22, off Istiklal Caddesi (0212 251 7020, www.jollyjokerbalans.com). **Open** 9pm-3am Mon-Thur; 10pm-4am Fri, Sat. **Map** p82 B3 **78**

The home of 'pop-rock' in Istanbul, Balans started out with huge ambitions and attracted huge international bands to its well-appointed stage. It's still a smart venue that occasionally pulls in global guests, but these days you're more likely to find local stars such as pop rocker Teoman and Eurovision Song Contest winner Sertab Erener.

Bigudi Pub

Istiklal Caddesi, Balo Sokak 20/ 4&5 (0555 835 1822, www.bigudi project.com). **Open** 2pm-2am daily. Club 10pm-5am Wed-Fri. **Map** p82 B3 **79**

Lipstick chic is the order of the evening at Istanbul's first lesbian bar. The terrace club is all girls; the café/pub, one floor below, is open to everyone LGBT, and friends.

Peyote

Kameriye Sokak 4, off Nevizade Sokak (0212 251 4398, www.peyote.com.tr). **Open** midnight-4am daily. **Map** p82 B3 **80**

Spread over several floors, this joint is a favourite of the city's alternative crowd. Each floor has a different vibe. And while it's well known for its live music, the open terrace on the roof is a popular place for drinks, before descending to the ground floor to enjoy the trance and electronica music from the resident DJ. Peyote also has a small performance space on the second floor, where various local bands play original material. With capacity limited to one hundred, it's the place to discover some of Istanbul's finest new talent. The beer is cheap, too.

Süheyla

Balık Pazarı, Galatasaray (0212 251 8347). **Open** 7pm-2am daily. No credit cards. **Map** p82 B3 **81**

A prime *fasıl* venue, nestled among the many restaurants in the Nevizade Sokak area, with two large rooms and above-average musicians. The set menu includes unlimited rakı for YTL60 per head. The place gets packed at weekends.

Taksim

If Çiçek Pasajı (see p100) represents old Beyoğlu, the new Beyoğlu is focused on the stretch of **Istiklal Caddesi** north of Galatasaray, which stretches all the way to **Taksim Square**. Here, arcades, churches and period architecture give way to malls, mega-stores and multiplexes, as well as endless bars and cafés.

At its north end, Istiklal Caddesi runs into Taksim Square. The giant square is one of the world's uglier plazas – little more than a snarled-up transport hub with a small park attached. Even so, the square is regarded as the heart of modern Istanbul and symbol of the secular Republic: its centrepiece is the **Independence Monument**, celebrating Kemal Atatürk's new republic.

Eating & drinking

There's a café or bar for every tribe – Africans, Anatolians, goths, bikers, students, intellectuals, gays and transvestites – around Taksim Square. Those in search of a cheap beer or a puff on a narghile loiter around **Mis Sokak** and **Büyük Parmakkapı Sokak**.

Gani Gani

Kuyu Sokak 13 (0212 244 8401, www.naumpasakonagi.com). **Open** 10am-midnight Mon-Thur, Sun; 10am-1am Fri, Sat. **$. Turkish.** **Map** p82 D3 ③

Popular with locals, this unusual eaterie buried in the backstreets near Taksim Square offers Anatolian eating at its best. Set on six floors, the place feels like a showcase for rural artefacts. Most of the seating – either in private

dining rooms or cosy communal spaces – is traditional Anatolian style, with low tables surrounded by kilims and cushions on the floor. Authentic eastern Turkish specialities include *çiğköfte* (à la turca steak tartare made with cracked wheat and chili), *mantı* (ravioli with yoghurt sauce), *pide* or *lahmacun* (Turkish-style pizzas), plus a range of kebabs. Narghiles (waterpipes) are available. No alcohol.

Kitchenette

NEW *Marmara Hotel, Taksim Square (0212 292 6862, www.kitchenette. com.tr).* **Open** 10am-10pm. **$$.** **French/Modern European.** **Map** p83 D2 ③

From the can-do-no-wrong Istanbul Doors Group, which also owns Anjelique and Vogue, this recent venture is brasserie, bakery, bar and breakfast joint. The space is stunning, with chrome booths and long wooden tables making for a large, but atmospheric, interior. The in-house bakery provides the bread for the large breakfasts, as well as to take away. There is also a wide selection of pastas, meat dishes and salads. It's not cheap, but for a long brunch in stylish surroundings it's worth it. There are Turkish wines by the glass (YTL13).

Mimolett

NEW *Sıraselviler Caddesi 55/A (0212 245 9858, www.mimolett.com.tr).* **Open** noon-3pm, 7pm-midnight Mon-Sat. *Bar* noon-2am Mon-Sat. **$$$$.** **Modern European.** **Map** p83 D3 ④

Murat Bozok worked at Michelin-starred restaurants in France and the UK (including a stint as head chef at Gordon Ramsay's Devonshire), before returning to his native city to open Mimolett, one of Istanbul's new breed of fine-dining restaurants. The menu is a Michelin-friendly selection of Modern European dishes; Turkish twists, seen in dishes such as a lamb chop and sweetbread dolma, bring originality and a sense of place. Quality is incredibly high, and the

ISTANBUL BY AREA

service flawless. The opulent yet modern interior befits a restaurant of this stature, but the terrace is the best place to take dinner, just as the sun sets and the moon rises over the Bosphorus. Mimolett also has a bar and wine shop.

Nature & Peace

Büyükparmakkapı Sokak 21-23 (0212 252 8609, www.natureandpeace.com). **Open** 11am-11.30pm Mon-Thur, Sun; 1-11.30pm Fri, Sat. **$$**. **Vegetarian**. **Map** p82 C3 ⑤

Vegetarian restaurants are rare in Istanbul, and even this pretender to the title serves several chicken dishes. The set lunch is great value and the dinner menu includes a soup and salad with any main course; pasta and falafel are reliable choices. One of the most popular dishes is a lentil 'meat-ball', with cabbage and nettle soup. The small, unpretentious space is cosy, if slightly musty.

Pia

Bekar Sokak 4A, off Istiklal Caddesi (0212 252 7100). **Open** 10am-2am daily. **Café/bar**. **Map** p82 C3 ⑥

The uncluttered decor and gallery-style mezzanine create a sense of space where there isn't much at all. Ornate mirrors and a single George Grosz print set the tone. This is a hang-out for writers, film-makers and other creative types. It's also the kind of place where single women will feel comfortable – in fact, some of the city's most beautiful women have been seen to drop into Pia. Dishes inspired by the owners' travels are served all day. The daily specials are usually worth a gamble.

Tokyo Restaurant

Ipek Sokak 1, off Istiklal Caddesi (0212 293 5858, www.tokyo-restaurant.com). **Open** 11am-11pm daily. **$$**. **Japanese**. **Map** p83 D3 ⑰

With its modern-traditional scarlet decor and tatami rooms, Tokyo is a hit with the local Japanese. The menu includes dozens of noodle, rice and teriyaki dishes, plus good sushi and sashimi. The sushi chefs show off their skills behind an open counter.

Topaz Restaurant

NEW *Ömer Avni Mahallesi, Inönü Caddesi 50, (0212 249 1001, www.topazistanbul.com).* **Open** noon-midnight daily. **$$$$**. **Modern Turkish/Mediterranean**. **Map** p83 F2 ⑱

Views from Topaz are superlative: picture windows run the length of the restaurant, which looks over the first Bosphorus bridge. The interior is comfortably modern, sleek and luxurious, and the food and service matches the look. Alongside the carte, there are two six-course *degustation* menus: the first is a modern interpretation of traditional Ottoman cuisine, with dishes such as artichoke with wild rice and grilled lamb loin with smoked aubergine purée. The second is a more modish Mediterranean selection, albeit with Turkish touches: cherry soup with shrimps and foam of rak and liquorish jelly, and oven-braised beef cheek with goose-liver crème brûlée, perhaps. All ingredients are rigorously sourced. The service is flawless, and the French sommelier can recommend Turkish or international wines. Cocktails are great too. Book ahead for a table by the window.

Zarifi

Çukurlu Çeşme Sokak 13 (0212 293 5480, www.zarifi.com.tr). **Open** 8pm-4am daily. **$$$**. Closed summer. **Turkish**. **Map** p82 C3 ⑲

An update on the *meyhane* that's very popular with fashionable young Turks. Zarifi's extensive menu covers all the classic meze and grilled meats, as well as Ottoman dishes and recipes inherited from the former Greek residents of the Pera neighbourhood, like shrimp *saganaki* and octopus stew. The soundtrack is equally eclectic – a mix of Turkish folk, chill-out tunes and mainstream pop. Once the *rakı* is flowing freely, the spirit of the *meyhane* usually takes over and spontaneous table-top dancing breaks out. This winning formula is duplicated every summer at Zarifi's supper club at the New Yorker in Kuruçeşme on the Bosphorus Shore.

Zencefil

Kurabiye Sokak 8 (0212 244 4082).
Open 11am-midnight Mon-Sat. **$.**
Vegetarian. Map p82 C2 ⑨

Probably the best vegetarian restaurant in Istanbul (though purists may be infuriated by the fact that chicken makes an occasional appearance on the menu). The setting is urban café meets country kitchen, with shelves lined with jars of produce and giant blackboards listing the daily specials, from soups to spicy stews and freshly baked breads. The home-style food is unfalteringly delicious, likewise the homemade lemonade.

Shopping

Mimolett (see p103) has a wine shop attached, stocking wines from Turkey's boutique vineyards.

Pandora

Büyükparmakkapı Sokak 3 (0212 243 3503, www.pandora.com.tr). **Open** 10am-8pm Mon-Wed; 10am-9pm Thur-Sat; 1-8pm Sun. Map p82 C3 ㉑

A fine little bookshop squeezed into three tight floors. The top one is filled with English-language titles, including fiction, poetry, art, local interest and a decent history section. Flyers and posters advertise events around town.

Nightlife

Jazz Café

Hasnün Galip Sokak 20, off Büyükparmakkapı Sokak (0212 245 0516, www.jazzcafeistanbul.com). **Open** 6pm-4am Mon-Sat. Closed July-mid Sept. Map p82 C3 ㉒

A dimly lit and cosy little venue allied to the 24-hour Jazz Café FM. Downstairs is a standard bar; upstairs is where the musicians perform to respectful silence. The main draw is veteran guitarist Bülent Ortaçgil, whose Wednesday night sessions have been going strong for ten years. His highly talented backing band includes fretless guitar maestro Erkan Oğur.

Klub Karaoke

Zambak Sokak 15 (0212 293 7639, www.klub-karaoke.com). **Open** 8pm-3am Mon-Thur, Sun; 8pm-5am Fri, Sat. Map p82 C3 ㉝

This karaoke club near Taksim Square consists of a small bar and two private rooms that are available for hire – the intimate, red-leather Tokyo Room and the larger, darker Fetish Room. Look out for theme nights dedicated to ladies, men, Turkish tunes or disco hits. Things don't really get going until around 11pm, then everyone wants a turn on the mic.

Mojo

Büyükparmakkapı Sokak 26, off Istiklal Caddesi (0212 243 2927, 243 2991, www.mojomusic.org). **Open** 10pm-4am daily. Map p82 C3 ㉞

A basement decorated with giant posters of rock 'n' roll legends, Mojo is the type of bar where long hair and leather jackets never go out of fashion. Istanbul has dozens of similar joints, including many more on this very street. Cover bands have struck chords and poses here every night of the week for almost a decade. Concerts usually begin around midnight.

Munzur

Hasnün Galip Sokak 21A (0212 245 4669). **Open** 6pm-4am daily. Map p82 C3 ㊟

From the outside, Munzur doesn't look that special. The inside is pretty nondescript too, but when the folk music starts this little bar suddenly becomes extraordinary. The outstanding quality of the musicians, who have a wicked way with a *bağlama*, is inspirational. Highly recommended.

Other Side
Zambak Sokak 2/5 (0212 235 7914). **Open** 8pm-3am daily. **Map** p82 C2 **96**
What used to be Istanbul's first gay restaurant is now a club, complete with house music, go-go boys and a tiny dancefloor. It's on the fourth floor of an apartment building, and decor is mist-matched and glitzy. The main bar is in the former living room and the back room is the place to discreetly make bedroom eyes at your new friend.

Privé
Tarlabaşı Bulvarı 28A (0212 235 7999). **Open** 11pm-5am daily.
Map p83 D2 **97**
An after-hours club that used to mix the slightly sordid with the upmarket, Privé was the place where minor celebrities and socialites could slum in safety. Recently, though, the more unsavoury elements appear to have taken over, with thuggish hustlers scaring off the better-heeled. Be thankful for the hulking bodyguards at the door – you may well need their help. The DJs shift a surprisingly progressive set.

Riddim
Sıraselviler Caddesi 69/1 (0212 251 2723, www.riddim.com.tr). **Open** 9pm-4am daily. **Map** p83 D3 **98**
Formerly the long-running Kemancı rock bar, this venue is an odd mixture of musical genres, with one floor devoted to rock, and another to hip hop and R&B. Locals seem to be loving it.

Roxy
Arslan Yatağı Sokak 3-7, off Sıraselviler Caddesi (0212 249 1283, 245 6539, www.roxy.com.tr). **Open** 9pm-3am Wed, Thur; 10pm-5am Fri, Sat. Closed July-Sept. **Map** p83 D4 **99**
Roxy used to be a major live venue, but its weekend club nights became so successful that the mainstream rock and pop bands have been relegated to the odd midweeker or an addendum to city-wide festivals. These live events are eclectic, with artists ranging from Luke Haines to Chumbawumba via Japanese 'acid mothers' Afrirampo. The place is usually packed with socia-ble, easy-going regulars, swigging bot-tled Sex On The Beach. Look out for the regular theme parties.

Arts & leisure

Akbank Culture & Arts Centre
Akbank Kültür ve Sanat Merkezi
İstiklal Caddesi 8 (0212 252 3500, www.akbanksanat.com). **Map** p82 C3 **100**
Opened in 1992 and fully renovated in 2001, this arts centre (better known as Akbank Sanat) boasts its own chamber music orchestra and a cosy, 135-seat, multi-purpose concert hall. The six-storey building hosts all sorts of cultural activities, from theatre to exhibitions to workshops.

Atatürk Cultural Centre (AKM)
Atatürk Kültür Merkezi
Taksim Square (0212 251 5600 box office, 0212 243 2011 or 251 1023 opera & ballet enquiries, www. idobale.com). No credit cards.
Map p83 E2 **101**
Istanbul's premier performing arts venue. Behind the brutalist 1960s design, the AKM is surprisingly grand and vibrant inside. There are two main concert halls, with a capacity of 1,300 and 520 a piece. Ticket prices are kept low through state subsidies. This hall is the most likely place to find Turkish classical music. The Türk Müziği chorus performs in the lower auditorium most Sundays from autumn to late spring. At the time of going to press, the venue was under renovation, and scheduled to reopen in 2011.

Bosphorus fusion

The Turkish chefs inspired by Istanbul's culinary culture.

Topaz

Istanbul is a city that stirs all the senses. But for many, it's the smell and taste of the food that makes the greatest impression.

Kebabs, fine fish and meze, accompanied with the anise-flavoured spirit *rakı*, remain perennially popular, but young Istanbul chefs are discovering a fusion cuisine that mixes fresh ingredients from the Bosphorus, spices from the bazaars and techniques learned in the restaurants of France, the US and UK. And this new generation of chefs have Michelin stars in their eyes.

At the forefront of the new Istanbul culinary movement is Murat Bozok, with his new restaurant, **Mimolett** (see p103). He is not the first to reinvent Turkish cuisine, but his antecedence is flawless: Pierre Gagnaire, Sketch, L'Atelier de Joel Robuchon in Paris, sous-chef at Petrus and head chef at Gordon Ramsay's Devonshire gastropub.

Mimolett has already garnered praise from the *New York*

Times and other international publications for dishes such as lamb chop and sweetbread *dolma*, in which French cooking styles are applied to indigenous ingredients; the menu is rounded out by some traditional French dishes, so you'll find foie gras sauté or a shrimp and truffle risotto on the menu too.

Murat is unequivocal about his ambition: 'I've always questioned why there isn't a Michelin star in Turkey,' Murat says. 'I'm determined to be the one.'

However, Murat is not the only chef cooking Michelin-friendly dishes in Istanbul today.

Nearby, in a stunning dining room with great views, is **Topaz** (see p104), a restaurant with two *degustation* menus: one traditional Ottoman and the other innovative Mediterranean. Topaz is one of Istanbul's best restaurants, and is known for using rigorously sourced Turkish ingredients and modern techniques.

Over at **Mikla** (see p91), meanwhile, Finnish-born head chef Mehmet Gurs, is blending Scandinavian and Turkish cuisine to great effect. Mikla's menu (and its views) make it another constant favourite among Istanbul's foodies.

Other modern culinary highspots include **Leb-i Derya** (see p96), along with **Changa** (Sıraselviler Caddesi 47, 0212 251 7064, www.changa-istanbul.com) and **Müzede Changa** (see p131), which is under the keen eye of New Zealand chef Peter Gordon, known worldwide for his fusion menus.

Beşinci Kat (5.Kat) p112

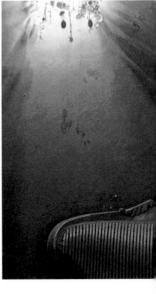

Çukurcuma

The side streets sloping south of Istiklal Caddesi's midpoint filter down into the appealingly decrepit district of **Çukurcuma**, whose twisting alleys are rife with fascinating antique and junk shops.

Eating & drinking

Cezayir

Hayriye Caddesi 12 (0212 245 9981, www.cezayir-istanbul.com). **Open** 9am-2am Mon-Thur, Sun; 9am-4am Fri, Sat. **Turkish/Bar**. Map p81 D1/p82 C4 **102**
Behind the Galatasaray Lycée, this fabulous 19th-century building was originally a school for the Italian Workers' Association. Beautifully converted into a glamorous bar and restaurant, Cezayir throngs with the city's literati and glitterati most nights of the week. The baroque silver and white dining room is stunning. The back room, with original floor tiles, soaring ceilings and a long wooden bar, is a stylish place for sharing some of the most inventive meze in Istanbul. There's a louche lounge with large mirrors and sofas, and a garden at the back that opens on to the twee restaurants of French Street.

Limonlu Bahçe

Yeniçarşı Caddesi 98 (0212 252 1094). **Open** *Nov-Mar* noon-11pm daily. *Apr-Oct* 9.30am-2am daily. **Bar**. Map p81 D2/p82 B4 **103**
Part-way down the precipitous slope of Yeniçarşı, Limonlu Bahçe is set in a big, bucolic back garden. This very pretty setting draws a self-conscious young crowd who loll around on cushions, flop in hammocks or gather around chunky wooden tables. There are plenty of tight T-shirts and cute tattoos on display. And if there aren't enough staff, nobody seems to mind.

Old City

Turnacı Başı Sokak 5/5, off Istiklal Caddesi (0212 244 28 96, www.old citycomedyclub.com). **Open** 8pm-midnight Mon-Thu; 8pm-4am Fri-Sat. **Bar**. Map p81 E1/p82 C4 **104**
Old City has been a late-night haunt of nocturnal Istanbullus for years. The place is a bit of a hit-or-miss affair. But on the right night, you're guaranteed shot-fuelled dancing or live cover bands until all hours. The best way to avoid the wrong night (and the occasional entrance fee) is to peek through the windows on Istiklal Caddesi: there's no mistaking if the joint is jumping. It's also a comedy club, but nearly always in Turkish.

Shopping

One of the best places for browsing, Çukurcuma's rollercoaster streets harbour a plethora of small shops with a wealth of antiquaria from rural Anatolia – anything from oil lamps and painted trunks to carved doors and tin toys. There's also a fair amount of sophisticated glass and porcelain ware, Ottoman screens and chandeliers. Among the dealers of carved wedding chests and period furniture are some dim, dusty cubbyholes that offer delightfully off-beat finds such as a temporary London bus stop or cigarette tins painted with scenes of Old Stamboul.

De Form Müzik

Turnacıbaşı Caddesi 45 (0212 245 3337). **Open** noon-8pm Mon-Sat; 1-7pm Sun. Map p81 D1/p82 C4 **105**
Vinyl fans need look no further. De Form, run by two friends, is an old-school music shop, with a turntable to test out your potential purchases. Most of the records here are Turkish editions of international artists, but there is a small selection of Turkish folk too. There is also dance music and, shhh, some CDs.

Retro fitted

Istanbul has caught the 20th-century bug.

The Works: Objects of Desire

Beyoğlu is no longer the rough, and slightly seedy, bohemia it once was. The boom in hip cafés and bars, exclusive restaurants and clubs has turned the district into the city's hottest destination for many Turks and visitors.

But open the doors of the city's best bars, and chances are it will be furnished with mid-century modern pieces, and accessorised with angle poise lamps, kitsch clocks and vintage film posters. Just visit **Lokal** (see p85), **KV Café** (see p85) or **Şimdi** (see p86) in Galata and **Meyra** (see p112) and **Smyrna** (see p114) in Cihangir for fine examples. The **House Café** chain (see box p84), designed by Autoban, follows the distinctive retro aesthetic to its pinnacle, with fabulous original furniture based on design classics of the 1950s through to the '70s.

There are few cities that seem to have embraced the retro aesthetic so wholeheartedly. The inspiration is understandable when wandering the labyrinth of steep, narrow streets in Çukurcuma,

where the city's antiques dealers, modern furniture sellers, artists' ateliers, and shops selling bric-a-brac from the last century can be found. Bostanbaşi Caddesi and Turnacı Başi Sokak are the best streets to start looking, but nothing beats spending an afternoon just wandering and getting lost.

To allow you to dress the part, **Leyla Seyhanli** (see right) and **Mozk** (see right) have hundreds of vintage items of clothing, including some unworn designer outfits.

For more eccentric pieces from the last century, try **The Works: Objects of Desire** (see right). Dubbed 'for the slightly deranged collector seeking identifiable memories', the shop has an eclectic selection of vintage kitchenware, old pornography, cash registers and pinball machines. Also on the premises at the time of writing were all manner of bits and pieces from a funfair – acquired when the owner bought the whole funfair. A similar shop is **Popcorn** (see right).

Eski Fener

Aga Hamam Sokak 77 (0212 251 6278). **Open** 11am-7pm Mon-Sat. No credit cards. **Map** p81 E1/p82 C4 ⑩⑥

A select assortment of furniture, doors, oil lamps and copperware, mostly picked up in rural Anatolia. There are things like low-legged dough-rolling tables, wooden butter churns and storm lamps. All items have been painstakingly restored.

Leyla Seyhanli

Altıpatlar Sokak 6 (0212 293 7410). **Open** 10am-7pm Mon-Sat. **Map** p81 E1/p82 C4 ⑩⑦

A massive selection of antique clothes, hats, embroidered linens, wall hangings and tapestries collected by Leyla Seyhanlı. Prices are quite high, but it's all top-quality stuff.

Mozk

Kuloğlu Mahallesi, Ağahamam Caddesi 13 (0212 252 3499, www.mozk.co.uk). **Open** 9am-9pm Mon-Sat. **Map** p81 E1/p82 C4 ⑩⑧

Run by two fashion designers, this vintage store exudes cool. Retro sunglasses, leatherwear, floral dresses, shirts, hats – just about any item of clothing, can be found in this little shop. Only items in excellent condition are sold. Some other vintage items, such as telephones, are available.

Popcorn

Faik Paşa Caddesi 2 (0212 249 5859). **Open** 10am-7pm Mon-Sat. No credit cards. **Map** p81 E1/p82 C4 ⑩⑨

This eclectic shop specialises in rare books, furniture and knick-knacks from the 1950s.

Porof Zihni Sinir

NEW *Kuloğlu Mahallesi Ağahamam Caddesi (0212 252 9320, www. zihnisinir.com).* **Open** 10am-7.30pm Mon-Sat. **Map** p81 E1/p82 C4 ⑩⑩

This remarkable store is at its core a toy shop, but the inventiveness of Irfan Sayar's creations could have found it a place in the Galleries chapter. Irfan is a cartoonist, whose character, a teacher called Porof Zihni Sinir, features in many Turkish children's books. However, his sculptures, at once tactile, fantastical and imaginative, have one thing in common: fun. Alongside the large-scale pieces, there are plenty of unique souvenirs and knick-knacks that would fit in a suitcase.

Sanatanik

Kuloğlu Mallahesi, Faikpaşa Caddesi 1/1 (532 372 8581). **Open** 10am-10pm daily. No credit cards. **Map** p81 E1/p82 C4 ⑪⑪

Friendly Aziz makes his own jewellery from antique beads. The folk pieces are inspired by a mix of Turkish and Central Asian infuences. Earrings, beautiful necklaces (some made from antique spoons) and wall decorations are part of the unique mix.

The Works: Objects of Desire

Faikpaşa Sokak 6/1 (0212 252 2527, www.fleaworks.com). **Open** 11am-6.30pm Mon-Sat. No credit cards. **Map** p81 E1/p82 C4 ⑪⑫

A remarkable shop that goes the extra mile in collecting the kitsch, the old and the downright bizarre. Owner Karaca Borar follows his own whims, and those of the collectors and film crews that buy and rent the goods. The shop, dubbed 'for the slightly deranged collector seeking identifiable memories', is stuffed with coats, hats, mannequins, old porn, unworn designer clothes, snow globes, and pretty much anything else. Prices are good, and as the sign says, 'no bargaining under YTL10, it's embarrassing'.

Cihangir

Rehabilitated from its dirty days as a shady part of town, Cihangir is now one of Istanbul's most coveted neighbourhoods. This transformation has been accompanied by the long overdue arrival of a decent selection of restaurants, and style-conscious cafés and bars catering to the area's predominantly arty and foreign residents. In warm weather, restaurants and cafés spread their tables out on to **Akarsu Caddesi** and stay open well into the small hours. At weekends, a leisurely brunch can easily last all day.

Eating & drinking

Beşinci Kat (5.Kat)

5th floor, Soğancı Sokak 3, off Sıraselviler Caddesi (0212 293 3774, www.5kat.com). **Open** 10am-2am Mon-Thur, Sun; 10am-3am Fri, Sat. **$$$. International.** Map p81 F1/p83 D4 ⑬

With its bright colours, velvet furnishings and an eye-catching floor piece of a nude young Norma Jean Baker, 5.Kat has one of the city's most striking interiors. As its name implies (*kat* means floor), it occupies the fifth floor of a back-street building. A giant neon angel shines at street level. A rooftop terrace, lit with red lanterns, opens during the summer and has fabulous views over the Asian Shore. The menu is a culinary mish-mash (Turkish, French, Italian, oriental) but everything is good. There are two fixed price menus, including two 'local' drinks, for YTL65 and YTL75. 5.Kat's actress proprietor, Yasemin Alkaya, keeps a close eye on proceedings, even after hours, when dance music takes over from chilled jazz, and the atmosphere gets clubby.

Cuppa

Yeni Yuva Sokak 22A (0212 249 5723, www.cuppajuice.com). **Open** 9am-9pm daily. **Juice bar.** Map p81 E2/p83 D5 ⑭

On one of the smaller streets behind Cihangir's main drag, this juice bar is the perfect antidote to Beyoğlu's boozy bars. Choose from around 40 fruit and veggie cocktails (YTL7-12), plus nutritious extras like wheatgrass, guarana or echinacea. The healthy menu extends to salads, wraps and sandwiches. The decor, like many places in the area is retro, with classic furniture, shelving holding up *National Geographic* magazines and *Peanuts* cartoon books, and a record player providing the tunes. Wi-Fi is available.

Doğa Balık

Akarsu Yokuşu Caddesi 46 (0212 243 3656). **Open** noon-midnight daily. **$$$. Turkish.** Map p81 E2/p83 D5 ⑮

Don't let the entrance, via the lobby of the Villa Zurich Hotel, put you off: Doğa Balık is a splendid neighbourhood fish restaurant. The dining room is on the seventh floor and is best known for its roof terrace, which has stunning views across to Sultanahmet and Beyoğlu. The cooking is equally impressive. The kitchen specialises in lightly cooked greens (up to 18 varieties) and perfectly grilled seasonal fish drizzled with garlicky olive oil. This is the quintessential Aegean comfort food – and it's good for you, too. On Wednesday, Friday and Saturday evenings there's live traditional music.

Meyra

Akarsu Caddesi 46 (0212 244 5350). **Open** 9am-4am daily. **$$. Café (licensed).** Map p81 E2/p83 D5 ⑯

Meyra (formerly Leyla) is a popular café that is unpretentiously cool. The retro designer furniture, chalkboard specials and airy interior with large windows opening on to street tables make it the perfect location for whiling away an afternoon. Menu highlights include all-day themed breakfasts, with geographical themes running from Istanbul to Oslo, Madrid and London. The English breakfast is a generous plate of bacon and eggs, with orange juice, tea and a selection of rolls. Salads, burgers and meat dishes are also available. There's wine by the glass and Efes beer is on tap. The bar is open late.

Meyra

Miss Pizza

*Hayvar Sokak 5, off Akarsu Caddesi
(0212 251 3279).* **Open** noon-midnight
daily (last orders 10.30pm). **$$**. **Pizza**.
Map p81 E2/p83 D5 **117**

Arguably the best pizzeria in town, this
stylish but cosy eatery in the heart of
Cihangir is a big hit with resident for-
eigners. Selen and Elif, who both have
backgrounds in textiles, were inspired
to create Miss Pizza by trips to Italy.
An Italian chef created the menu and
taught them to make pizza dough.
Pizza *funghi*, made with gorgonzola
and porcini mushrooms marinated in
truffle oil, is our recommendation.
Besides pizza, there are good cheese
and charcuterie platters and salads.
There are only a few tables, but you
can also order home delivery.
Reservations are essential on Fridays
and Saturdays.

Smyrna

Akarsu Caddesi 29 (0212 244 2466).
Open 9am-4am daily. **$$**. **Café
(licensed)**. **Map** p81 E2/p83 D5 **118**

Traditionally, Cihangir's favourite
hangout has been the cluster of tea
houses by the mosque, where local
loafers can spend a whole day or
evening ensconced beneath the plane
trees, nursing a dirt-cheap glass of tea.
Nearby Smyrna is where the tea house
regulars come when they're feeling
flush, to rub shoulders with the actors
and artists who live in the area. The
fabulous decor has been assembled
from junk shops of the area and is a
mix of the antique, modern and downright whimsical. Food includes salads,
pastas and meat dishes. Laid-back
enough for daytime lounging and
lunching, Smyrna shifts up a few
gears after dark.

Susam Café

Susam Sokak 11 (0212 251 5995).
Open 9am-2am daily. **Café
(licensed)**. **Map** p81 F2/p83 D5 **119**

Quaint little Susam has a menu with
hot and cold coffees, teas, freshly
squeezed juices, lemonade, cookies,
cakes and other sweets. There are
waffles and pancakes too. Mains
include toasts, salads, sandwiches,
meat and chicken. There's food to take
away, too.

Shopping

Antre Gourmet Shop

*Akarsu Caddesi 52 (0212 292 8972,
www.antregourmet.com).* **Open** 9am-
9pm Mon-Sat; 9am-8pm Sun. **Map** p81
E2/p82 C5 **120**

Antre stocks around 40 regional
cheeses, all bought from local producers and free from additives. There's
also a fair selection of cold meats, along
with Austrian wholegrain breads, teas,
home-made meze dishes and jams.
Olive oil, honeycomb (in season),
Turkish wines and natural yoghurt are
also stocked.

Berrin Akyüz

*Akarsu Caddesi 20 (0212 251 4125,
www.berrinakyuz.com).* **Open** 10am-
8pm Mon-Fri; 10am-5pm Sat-Sun.
Map p81 E2/p83 D5 **121**

Designer Berrin Akyüz works half her
time in her atelier in Üsküdar and half
time in this Cihangir shop, which sells
her skirts, tops, scarves, bags,
children's wear and jewellery. She
works with Polish designer Lucasz
Budzisz, who specialises in corsets,
and between them they offer four
collections every year.

La Cave

*Sıraselviler Caddesi 109A (0212 243
2405, www.lacavesarap.com).* **Open**
9am-9pm Mon-Sat; 9am-8pm Sun.
Map p81 E1/p82 C4 **122**

One of the city's first speciality wine
shops, and certainly the most serious.
Owner Esat Ayhan keeps a comprehensive cellar filled with wines from all
over Turkey, Europe and the New
World. He also stocks imported spirits,
bar accessories and a limited range of
Havana cigars.

Savoy Pastanesi

*Sıraselviler Caddesi 181 (0212 249
1818, www.savoypastanesi.com).*
Open 7am-10.30pm daily. **Map**
p81 E1/p82 C4 ⑫③

One of Istanbul's best cake shops, and
now something of an institution.
There's a reasonably sized café up on
the first floor, which gets especially
busy at breakfast.

Nightlife

Andon

*Sıraselviler Caddesi 89 (0212 251
0222, www.andon.com.tr).* **Open** 7pm-
5am daily. **Map** p81 E1/p82 C4 ⑫④

A four-storey multi-purpose venue
close to Taksim. As well as being a
meyhane, it's equipped with a wine
bar, terrace restaurant and disco bar,
not to mention Bosphorus views,
accomplished musicians and smart
service. The dimly lit interior creates
a flattering backdrop for the dressed-
up diners. A good place to start
exploring *fasıl* if you're not ready to
jump in at the deep end.

Karaköy

Karaköy has been a port since
Byzantine times, when the north
shore of the Golden Horn was
a separate settlement – Galata
– distinct from the rest of
Constantinople. Much of the
maritime traffic has since moved
out and the area is being cleaned
up, but it still has several
monuments reflecting its grittier
past. Today, the **Istanbul
Modern** gallery is the area's
main draw for visitors.

Karaköy has a refreshingly
diverse array of religious
monuments. As well as the
Yeraltı Mosque and **Jewish
Museum**, there are a couple of
curious churches. The **Russian
Orthodox Church of St
Andrea** on Balyoz Sokak is
on the top floor of what appears
to be a 19th-century apartment
building, but was actually built
as a monastery. The monks have
long gone, but the church has
experienced a revival thanks to
the Russian tourists who have
arrived en masse since the collapse
of the Soviet Union. Around the
corner is the **Church of St
Panagia**, belonging to the tiny
Turkish Orthodox sect, which
broke away from the Greek church
in the 1920s. Mass here is said in
the Karamanlı Turkish dialect.

North along **Kemeraltı
Caddesi**, the road passes in the
shadow of the slightly sinister
Tophane. A former Ottoman
cannon foundry built during the
reign of Mehmet the Conqueror,
the current building, with its
distinctive row of ventilation
towers, only dates to 1803.
Recently renovated, it's now
used as an occasional arts and
exhibition centre.

Opposite are two impressive
mosques. **Kılıç Ali Paşa Mosque**
was built in 1580 by the celebrated
architect Sinan. A little further
north is **Nusretiye Mosque**,
built in the late 1820s in baroque
style by Kikor Balyan, an
Armenian architect whose sons
would later design the nearby
Dolmabahçe Palace (see p126).
Behind the mosque is a row of
cafés specialising in narghiles
(see box p55).

Sights & museums

Istanbul Modern

*Meclis-i Mebusan Caddesi, Liman
İşletmeleri Sahası, Antrepo No.4
(0212 334 7300, www.istanbul
modern.org). Tram Karaköy.*
Open 10am-6pm Tue, Wed, Fri-Sun;
10am-8pm Thur. **Admission** YTL8;
YTL3 reductions. Free for all Thur.
Map p81 E3 ⑫⑤

Created as Turkey's equivalent of London's Tate Modern, Istanbul Modern has grown comfortably into its role since opening in 2004. Housed in a former customs warehouse on the waterfront in Karaköy, the two-storey museum has 8,000 square metres of exhibition space. The permanent collection follows the transformation of Turkish art since the foundation of the Academy of Fine Arts in 1893 and reflects Turkey's shifting economic and political landscape.

On entering the unremarkable building, you'll see a large, site-specific piece from the eighth Biennial – a shattered glass staircase hung from steel chains, created by Monica Bonvicini. And similarly, Richard Wentworth's installation of hundreds of books suspended over the library, for the Centre of Gravity exhibition, proved so popular that it stayed.

The Lower Floor Galleries house temporary exhibitions. These have introduced major international artists, including Anish Kapoor, Juan Munoz and William Kentridge, to a local audience. However, Turkish artists are getting more space than they have in the past with shows from the likes of photographer Pınar Yolaç and painter Burhan Uygur.

One of the museum's galleries is dedicated exclusively to photography; another is devoted to video art. The in-house cinema screens an interesting mix of Turkish and international arthouse movies and experimental shorts.

The museum's restaurant has proved a big hit in its own right. Stunning views across the Bosphorus to the minarets of Sultanahmet and out to the Marmara Sea just about justify bumped-up prices for decent bistro fare.

Jewish Museum
Türk Musevileri Müzesi
Karaköy Meydanı, Perçemli Sokak (0212 292 6333, www.muze500.com). Tram Karaköy. **Open** 10am-4pm Mon-Thur, 10am-2pm Fri, Sun. **Admission** YTL7. No credit cards. **Map** p80 C5 ⓰

Housed in the immaculately restored Zülfaris Synagogue (in existence since 1671, but dating in its present form to the early 19th century), a collection of well-presented objects, documents, photographs and storyboards (in English) tells the story of over 500 years of Jewish presence in Turkey. The Jews first arrived in the Ottoman Empire fleeing the pogroms of Christian Europe. They have made significant contributions to Istanbul life, particularly in the financial sector. An ethnography section presents costumes and accessories related to circumcision ceremonies, dowries and weddings.

Yeraltı Mosque
Yeraltı Camii
Kemankeş Cadessi. Tram Karaköy. **Open** varies. **Admission** free. **Map** p80 C5 ⓱

Often called the Underground Mosque because it's buried beneath a 19th-century wooden mansion, the low, vaulted interior of the Yeraltı Mosque is supported by 54 columns, built on the remains of the Byzantine castle of Galata, which guarded the entrance to the Golden Horn. From here, a great chain was stretched across the waterway, blocking access to enemy ships in times of siege. The upper part of the castle was demolished following the Ottoman conquest, and the remaining lower floor – formerly a prison – was converted to a mosque in 1757.

Shopping

Güllüoğlu
Mumhane Caddesi 171 (0212 293 0910, www.karakoygulluoglu.com). Tram Karaköy. **Open** 7am-10pm Mon-Sat. **Map** p81 D4 ⓲

Güllüoğlu is the king of baklava and *su boreği* (baked layers of cheese, fresh herbs and filo pastry).

Fatih Pazarı p121

Beyond the Centre

West

The sprawling Western Districts are a collection of old neighbourhoods that make up some of the most religious areas in the city. In **Fatih**, **Fener** and **Balat**, headscarves, chadors and the baggy *şalvar* trousers worn by devout men are much in evidence.

Often neglected by visitors, the area is rich in atmosphere and monuments, peppered with synagogues, churches and Greek Orthodox schools, as well as some impressive mosques – a reminder that until early last century, around 40 per cent of the population were Christians and Jews.

Highlights in this area are the **Church of St Saviour in Chora**, one of the city's foremost Byzantine monuments, and, a mile beyond the remains of the Byzantine **city walls**, the holiest mosque in Istanbul, **Eyüp Sultan Mosque**.

Sights & museums

Blachernae Palace
Anemas Zindanları
Ivaz Ağa Caddesi, Ayvansaray. Bus 5T, 99A. **Open** 9am-7pm daily. **Admission** YTL2.
Constructed around AD 500, the palace was extended in the 11th and 12th centuries, by which time it had become the favoured imperial residence. It's now mostly in ruins. The best-preserved sections are the brick and marble three-storey façade, the Palace of the Porphyrogenitus and, below the Ahmet tea garden, the five floors of tunnels and galleries that were cleared of rubble in 1999 for a film shoot and are rather awesome in their medieval splendour.

Cartoon Museum
Karikatür ve Mizah Müzesi
Kavacılar Sokak 12, off Atatürk Bulvarı, Şehzadebaşı (0212 521 1264). Tram Laleli or Üniversite. **Open** 9am-5pm Tue-Sat. **Admission** free.

Set in a beautiful 17th-century *medrese*, this is one of the city's more unusual museums. Where instructors once lectured students in Islamic philosophy, they now give lessons in illustration, engraving and screen-printing. The permanent collection, with pieces dating back to the 1870s, illustrates the long-standing popularity of caricature and satire in Turkey. One recurring theme is the insidious influence of the West.

Church of St Saviour in Chora
Kariye Müzesi

Kariye Camii Sokak 26, Edirnekapı (0212 631 9241). Metro Ulubatlı or bus 37E, 38E, 91O to Vefa Stadium. **Open** 9am-5pm Mon, Tue, Thur-Sun. **Admission** YTL15.

For Byzantine splendour, this church (also known as the Kariye Mosque or Museum) is second only to Haghia Sophia. Built in the late 11th century, its celebrated mosaics and frescoes were added when the church was remodelled in the 14th century. Depicting all manner of Christian themes, from the Day of Judgement through to the Resurrection, the works here are arguably the most important surviving examples of Byzantine art in the world, both in terms of their execution and preservation.

Church of Surp Hreşdagabet (Holy Angels)

Kamış Sokak, Balat. Bus 35D. **Open** *Services* Thur am. **Admission** free.

Tentatively dated to the 13th century, this church was taken over by the Armenians in the early 17th century. Although much of the current structure dates from 1835, the side chapel and *ayazma* (sacred spring) are original Byzantine features.

City walls

Constructed in the reign of Theodosius II (408-450), the walls of Constantinople are the largest Byzantine structure that survives in modern Istanbul. These walls withstood invading armies for over 1,000 years, resisting siege on more than 20 occasions until the Ottoman conquest in 1453.

The walls encompass the old city in a great arc, and stretch for some 6.5 kilometres (four miles) from the Golden Horn to the Sea of Marmara. Together with the sea walls that ringed Constantinople, these walls constituted Europe's most extensive medieval fortifications.

Walking the walls

There are several ways to get to the walls, depending on which part you want to visit. It's possible to walk the whole length, along both the inside and outside, although care should be taken as some sections are deserted apart from vagrants. The best place to begin is on the Marmara coast at Yedikule. Take a bus from Eminönü (80) or Taksim (80T) or, for a more scenic ride, a suburban train from Sirkeci to Yedikule. The train passes under the ramparts of Topkapı Palace and winds in and out of what remains of the southern sea walls.

On the Marmara shore, the walls begin with the imposing Marble Tower on a promontory by the sea. It has served as both an imperial summer pavilion and as a prison. You can still see the chute through which executed corpses were dumped into the sea.

On the other side of the coastal road is the near-pristine Gate of Christ, the first of 11 fortified gates. On the northern side of the railway line is Yedikule Fortress, whose entrance is in the north-east wall.

Approaching the Golden Horn, the city walls end at the Byzantine Blachernae Palace (see p117).

Eyüp Sultan Mosque
Eyüp Sultan Camii

Eyüp Midanı, off Camil Kebir Caddesi. Ferry from Eminönü. **Open** 9am-6pm daily. **Admission** free.

The holiest mosque in Istanbul's status comes from being the (reputed) burial place of Eyüp Ensari, companion and standard-bearer of the Prophet Muhammad. His tomb is adjacent to the mosque and has a gold-framed footprint of Muhammad and some fancy Iznik tiling. A vast *külliye* (complex) surrounds the mosque, with most buildings dating to 1458. Non-Muslims are welcome, but visitors should dress modestly. Headscarves are available.

Fatih Mosque
Fatih Camii
Fevzi Paşa Caddesi. Metro Emmyet.
Open 9am-dusk daily. **Admission** free.
The grounds of Fatih Mosque are a popular place for pious picnickers. The vast 18th-century baroque structure is built on the site of the Church of the Holy Apostles, burial place of most Byzantine emperors, including Constantine. The church was already in ruins by the time Mehmet II conquered Constantinople. He used it as a quarry for a mosque built in 1470 to celebrate his victory (*fatih* means 'conqueror'). Most of Mehmet's original structure was destroyed by an earthquake in 1766; all that remains is the courtyard and parts of the main entrance. The tomb of the Conqueror stands behind the prayer hall.

Panorama 1453 History Museum
Topkapı Culture Park, Merkez Efendi Mahallesi, Topkapı (212 467 0700, www.panoramikmuze.com). Tram Topkapı. **Open** 9am-8pm daily.
Admission YTL10.
See box p122.

Santralistanbul
Eski Silahtaraga Elektrik Santrali, Istanbul Bilgi Üniversitesi, Kazım Karabekir Caddesi 1, Silahtar (0212 311 5000, www.santralistanbul.com). Bus 44B. **Open** 10am-8pm daily.
Admission YTL7.
See box right.

The power of art

Istanbul's most exciting arts venue.

It's no longer surprising to find art galleries in converted industrial buildings; think of Tate Modern in London and galleries across Germany's Ruhr Valley. Not only is it a creative solution to industrial decline, but old factories also make very good gallery spaces. The cavernous buildings are a clean slate.

Santralistanbul (see left) is a prime example of a cutting-edge arts and cultural complex in an industrial setting. Within the concrete walls of this former power station, the first in the Ottoman Empire, are a 7,000-square-metre modern art gallery, an amphitheatre, concert halls and a public library. Its multidisciplinary approach has covered subjects including architecture and photography as well as showing retrospectives of artists such as photographer Martin Parr and political painter Yüksel Arslan.

There's also an impressive concert space that attracts innovative artists such as Cinematic Orchestra and the Gorillaz Sound System, as well as electronic artists and a healthy jazz programme.

SantralIstanbul is closely tied to the Istanbul Bilgi University, with its School of Architecture leading the conversion of the former power plan. The university also contributes to exhibitions.

Kanyon p124

Şehzade Mosque
Şehzade Camii

Şehzadebaşı Caddesi, Saraçhane, Şehzadebaşı. Tram Üniversite or Laleli. **Open** 9am-dusk daily. **Admission** free.
Completed in 1548, Sinan dismissed his first royal mosque complex as 'apprentice work'. It is named after Prince Sehzade Mehmet, son of Süleyman, who died suddenly and prematurely. He is buried in the complex. The square courtyard is as big as the interior of the mosque. The combination of the square plan and the central dome surrounded by four half domes is unprecedented in Islamic architecture.

Yedikule Fortress
Yedikule Müzesi

Yedikule Meydanı Sokak, Yedikule (0212 585 8933). Yedikule Station from Sirkeci or bus 80, 80T. **Open** 8am-5pm Mon, Tue, Thur-Sun. **Admission** YTL5.
Impressively restored, this Byzantine 'Castle of the Seven Towers' was remodelled by the Ottomans. Its western face incorporates the Golden Gate (now bricked up), a triumphal arch erected around AD 390. The vertiginous battlements offer wonderful views.

Eating & drinking

These relatively poor, religiously conservative parts of town get few visitors, so there's little call for restaurants.

Asitane
Kariye Hotel, Kariye Camii Sokak 18, Edirnekapı (0212 534 8414, www.asitanerestaurant.com). Bus 28, 77MT, 87. **Open** 11.30am-11pm daily. **$$. Turkish.**
It may be a trek to Edirnekapı, but it's worth it for this one-of-a-kind restaurant, which specialises in authentic Ottoman food. Authentic means just that: the same dishes that were served at the circumcision feasts of Sultan Süleyman's sons, Beyazıd and Cihangir,

in 1539. Expect lots of sweet and sour fruit and meat combos: *kavun dolması* is melon stuffed with mincemeat, rice, almonds, currants and pistachios; *nirbaç* is a stew made with diced lamb, meatballs and carrots, spiced with coriander, ginger, cinnamon, pomegranate and crushed walnuts. The leafy garden is lovely in summer.

Pierre Loti
Balmumcu Sokak 5, off Gümüşsuyu Caddesi (0212 581 2696). Bus 55ET. **Open** 8am-midnight daily. No credit cards. **Café.**
On a hilltop with a stunning vantage point over the Golden Horn, this café is dedicated to French naval officer and romantic novelist Pierre Loti, who was so obsessed with Istanbul that he took to masquerading as a Turk and remodelled his house as a 'sultan's palace'. Legend has it Loti would sit at this spot for hours, gazing over the city and gathering inspiration for his literary masterpiece, *Aziyade*. To get here, climb up through the scenic cemetery near Eyüp Mosque or take a cable car.

Shopping

Fatih Pazarı
Darüşşafaka Caddesi, Fatih. **Open** Wed.
This vast open-air market surrounds the Fatih Mosque and fills its rambling courtyard. Join the headscarved crowds to tussle over leopard-print lingerie, surplus clothing and household items. It also has an excellent reputation for food: expect to find top village produce, including local cheeses, baskets of fresh roseships and, in season, cornelian cherries.

North

North of Taksim, there is little to capture the visitor's imagination in the residential neighbourhoods of **Harbiye** and **Şişli**, save for a couple of museums celebrating Turkey's military conquests and

The fall of the city

Watch as Istanbul's most dramatic day unfolds.

The year 1453 was one of the most significant in Istanbul's history. The Byzantines had held the city since circa AD 330, but by the 14th century the Ottomans had conquered most of western Asia Minor and advanced as far as Bulgaria. Constantinople had become a Byzantine island in an Ottoman sea.

By April 1453, Ottoman forces surrounding Constantinople numbered some 80,000; facing them were just 5,000 men. In an audacious move, the Ottomans circumvented a great chain that had been stretched across the Bosphorus by hauling 70 ships on rollers up over the ridge above Galata and down to the water on the other side. By dawn the city had fallen. The Ottoman empire had a new capital.

This dramatic event is now the subject of the **Panorama 1453 History Museum** (see p119), which displays the battle on a dazzling 2,350sq m panoramic painting. Accompanied by the sounds of the Janissaries' band, the cries of soldiers and the thunder of cannon shot, the multimedia show is one of the more visceral ways to experience the event. The detail in the painting, which took three years to produce, is phenomenal and costumes historically accurate. In a neat twist, the museum is located by Topkapı Gate, where the Ottomans first breached the city.

republican ideals. Şişli, however, could be the next neighbourhood to become trendy, with restaurants, shops and boutique hotels opening.

For a different take on Istanbul's bar life, head up to **Nişantaşı** or **Teşvikiye**, a pair of upper-class neighbourhoods north of Taksim with a lively bar scene, designer boutiques and equally swanky eateries. Further from the centre, **Levent** and **Etiler**, a couple of Istanbul's wealthier business districts – comprising glass skyscrapers, monolithic malls and bumper-to-bumper SUVs – are home to a clutch of fine restaurants.

Sights & museums

Atatürk Museum
Atatürk Müzesi
Halaskargazi Caddesi 250, Şişli (0212 240 6319). Bus 46H or metro Osmanbey. **Open** 9am-4pm Wed, Fri-Sun. **Admission** free.
In northern Şişli, a short bus ride from Taksim Square, is a candy-pink Ottoman house in which Mustafa Kemal once stayed. It now contains three floors of memorabilia of the great Atatürk, from his astrakhan hat to his silk underwear. There's even a wine-stained tablecloth on which he bashed out the new Turkish alphabet over a picnic lunch in 1928. The top floor holds a large collection of propaganda paintings from the War of Independence.

Military Museum
Askeri Müze ve Kültür Sitesi
Vali Konağı Caddesi, Harbiye (0212 233 2720). Bus 46H, 46KY, 69YM or metro Osmanbey. **Open** 9am-4.30pm Wed-Sun. **Admission** YTL3. No credit cards.
The sheer size and wealth of this place says as much about the military's continued clout in Turkey as it does about the country's bloody history. Definitely worth seeing are the gloriously colourful campaign pavilions of the Ottoman

sultans, created from embroidered silk and cotton. Upstairs, in the 20th-century section, there's a decent display dealing with the 1915 Gallipoli campaign, plus some bizarre furniture constructed out of bayonets and gun parts. For sheer morbidity, nothing beats the car in which the Grand Vizier Mahmut Şevket Paşa was assassinated while travelling along Divan Yolu in 1913.

Rahmi M Koç Museum
Rahmi M Koç Müzesi
Hasköy Caddesi 27, Hasköy (0212 369 6600, www.rmk-museum.org.tr). Bus 47, 54HM, 54HT. **Open** 10am-5pm Tue-Fri; 10am-7pm Sat, Sun. **Admission** YTL10. *Submarine* YTL4. No credit cards.
This converted 18th-century foundry is a showcase for the assorted obsessions of one of the wealthiest men in Turkey. The collection includes hall after hall of antique trains, trams, boats and planes. There's even a submarine moored in the Golden Horn. Many exhibits have moving parts that can be activated by buttons or levers; there's a walk-on ship's bridge with a wheel, sonar machines and alarm bells. Try to visit on a Saturday or Sunday, when all the working models are in action.

Eating & drinking

Halat
Kumbarhane Caddesi 2, Hasköy (0212 297 6644). Bus 47E, 54HT. **Open** 10am-midnight Tue-Sun. **$$**. *French*.
In addition to being a world-class museum, the Rahmi Koç has a couple of excellent restaurants in the Café du Levant, a fancy French bistro, and Halat, with quayside dining under canvas awnings. The menu ranges from a 'tea-time' selection of sandwiches and tarts to breaded crab claws and heavenly desserts. Black-waistcoated staff and classical music suggest formality, but the vibe is laid-back. The views – across the Golden Horn to the tumbling orange roofs of Balat – are stunning.

Hünkar
Mim Kemal Öke Caddesi 21 (0212 225 4665). Metro Osmanbey. **Open** noon-midnight daily. **$**. **Turkish**.
The original Hünkar opened in 1950 in the working-class Fatih neighbourhood; this offshoot in Nişantaşı has taken the old-school Ottoman brand upmarket. Diners include Chanel-suited ladies who lunch and businessmen who schmooze over homely dishes such as sheep's trotter soup, stuffed cabbage, anchovy pilaf, or the signature dish *hünkar beğendi* – 'sultan's delight' – a rich lamb stew with aubergine purée.

Longtable
Sofa Hotel, Teşvikiye Caddesi 123 (0212 224 8181, www.thesofahotel.com). Metro Osmanbey. **Open** 7pm-2am Mon-Sat. **$$$**. **Modern Turkish**.
The interior design is eclectic and light-hearted, bordering on the kitsch, with a catwalk-like walkway running down the centre of the restaurant, parallel to the bar – the 'longtable' of the name. The menu majors in dry-aged meat: veal medallions, New York steak and 23 types of seasoned ribeye steaks. There are also chicken and fish selections, salads, pizzas and pastas. There's live soul music 9-11pm Tue-Sat.

Naz Turkish Cuisine
Swissôtel The Bosphorus, Bayıldım Caddesi 2, Maçka (0212 326 1175, www.nazturk.com). **Open** 11.30am-midnight daily. **$$$**. **Turkish**.
Housed in a model of an 18th-century *yalı* (mansion) next to the Swissôtel in Maçka, Naz serves traditional Ottoman cuisine. Avoiding any ostentatious faux-Ottoman decor, the interior is austere. Aimed at tourists and business people, the food offers an introductory selection of superior mezes. The signature main course is *kuzu kafes* for two (YTL95), which is lamb with fig-flavoured potatoes, grilled baby squash and two sauces. Live music often accompanies dinner.

Salomanje

Belkıs Apartmanı 4/1-2, Atiye Sokak
(0212 327 3577). Metro Osmanbey.
Open 11.30am-2am Mon-Sat. Closed
summer. **$$**. **Modern European**.
This café-restaurant is a hit with
Nişantaşı's stylish residents, although
entering the tiny spot you may wonder
why. With a bar, a handful of tables and
a small rear terrace, the decor is unre-
markable but cosy. The menu combines
Turkish and international standards.

Sunset Grill & Bar

Yol Sokak 2, off Adnan Saygun
Caddesi, Ulus Parkı, Ulus (0212 287
0357, www.sunsetgrillbar.com). Metro
Levent. **Open** noon-3pm, 7pm-2am
daily. **$$$$**. **International**. *Metro*
A gorgeous setting for a romantic tryst
– a tree-lined terrace set on a hilltop
high above the Bosphorus. The menu
is an unlikely but well-executed mix of
Californian fusion, meat-heavy modern
Turkish dishes and superior sushi. It's
hugely popular at sunset – book ahead.

Ulus 29

Kireçhane Sokak 1, Adnan Saygun
Caddesi, Ulus Parkı, Ulus (0212 265
6181, www.group-29.com). Metro
Levent. **Open** noon-3pm, 7pm-midnight
daily. **$$$$**. **Mediterranean**.
Someone to impress? Something to cel-
ebrate? Ulus 29 fits the bill. Thanks to
yet another spectacular hillside setting
(just above the Sunset Grill & Bar), the
views from the semi-circular verandah
are unbeatable. Models make eyes at
moguls against an opulent Oriental
backdrop, decked with muslin drapes
and lit by oil lamps. Food is impressive,
focusing on the eastern Mediterranean.

Shopping

There are lots of malls and
department stores here. In addition
to those listed below, there is
Akmerkez (www.akmerkez.
com.tr), an upmarket mall whose
250 shops include posh department

store **Beymen**, and giant **Cevahir**
(www.istanbulcevahir.com), directly
linked to Metro Şişli and home to a
branch of **YKM** (www.ykm.com.tr),
Turkey's oldest department store.

Gönül Paksoy

Atiye Sokak 1/3, Teşvikiye (0212 261
9081). Metro Osmanbey. **Open** 1-7pm
Mon; 10am-7pm Tue-Sat.
Ms Paksoy's collections reinterpret
Ottoman designs, using original fabrics
and the finest natural weaves hand-
dyed in subtle shades. She also does a
great line in Ottoman-style slippers,
handbags and shoes.

Kanyon

Büyükdere Caddesi 185, Levent (0212
353 5300, www.kanyon.com.tr). Metro
Levent. **Open** 10am-10pm daily.
Kanyon is a mall with a difference.
Open to, yet sheltered from, the ele-
ments, it houses 170 boutiques, a
plethora of restaurants – including
branches of Kitchenette and House
Café (see box p85), and the plushest cin-
ema in town. Shopping-wise, the accent
is on prestige fashion and lifestyle
labels, both local and foreign: the likes
of Harvey Nichols, Georg Jensen,
Swarovski and department store
Vakko (www.vakko.com.tr).

Metrocity

Büyükdere Caddesi 171, Levent (212
344 0660, www.metrocity.com.tr).
Metro Levent. **Open** 10am-10pm daily.
Like Kanyon across the road, this four-
storey mall is served by a direct link to
the metro. What's different is that it
pitches to a far more middle-of-the-road
clientele. Among the 140 stores, you'll
find Marks & Spencer vying for busi-
ness with Benetton, Zara, Mavi Jeans
and the like.

Nelia

Halil Bey Pasajı 40/19, off Valikonağı
Caddesi, Nişantaşı (0216 451 7438,
www.nelia.com.tr). Metro Osmanbey.
Open 10am-7.30pm Mon-Sat.

Nelia produces funky, chunky jewellery with a tribal twist. Its designer works with a multitude of materials, crafting weird and wonderful combinations.

Urart

Abdi İpekçi Caddesi 18/1, Nişantaşı (0212 246 7194, www.urart.com.tr). Metro Osmanbey. **Open** 9am-7pm Mon-Sat.
Sophisticated jewellery whose designs are drawn from the countless civilisations to have peopled Anatolia up to Ottoman times, using a combination of silver, gold and semi-precious stones.

Zeki

Akkavak Sokak 47/9, Tunaman Çarşısı, Nişantaşı (0212 233 8279, www. zekitriko.com.tr). Metro Osmanbey. **Open** 9.30am-7.30pm Mon-Sat.
Not only is Zeki the premier swimwear label at home, it's also one of Turkey's most successful exports. Prices are high, but so is the quality. Check out the own-label lingerie.

Nightlife

Despina

Açıkyol Sokak 9, Kurtuluş (0212 232 6720). Bus 70KE, 70KY. **Open** noon-midnight daily.
With its fluorescent lights and plastic flowers, Despina doesn't look promising. But fine musicians play here, drawing a demonstrative audience, who submit requests for their favourite *oyun havaları* (dance songs). On the right night, this can be the best party in town.

Love

Cumhuriyet Caddesi 349/1, Harbiye (0212 296 3357). **Open** 11.30pm-4am Tue-Thur; 11.30pm-5am Fri, Sat.
Istanbul's only gay venue worthy of the title 'club', Love Point has a full-size dancefloor, a no riff-raff door policy, professional sound system and groovy DJs. It draws a mixed crowd, most of whom are too focused on dancing and preening to notice anyone else.

Arts & leisure

Büyük Hamam

Potiniciler Sokak 22, Kasımpaşa, Beyoğlu (0212 238 9800 men, 0212 256 9835 women). **Open** *Men* 5.30am-10.30pm daily. *Women* 9am-7pm daily. No credit cards.
This no-frills hamam is favoured by locals. The name means 'the big bathhouse' – indeed, this is Istanbul's largest. The beautiful details are courtesy of the Ottoman architect Sinan (also responsible for the mosque next door). An open-air swimming pool has been added to the men's section.

Cemal Reşit Rey Concert Hall
Cemal Reşit Rey Konser Salonu

Darülbedai Caddesi 1, Harbiye (0212 232 9830, www.crrks.org). Bus 43, 46Ç, 46ÇY, 46H, 46KY.
This venue, the 860-seat home of the municipal CRR Symphony Orchestra, has a diverse programme, including Turkish religious, classical and traditional music. It's a key venue for several festivals. Tickets also available from www.biletix.com.

İş Art & Culture Centre
İş Sanat Kültür Merkezi

İş Towers (İş Kuleleri), Kule 1 17, Levent (0212 316 1083, www. issanat.com.tr). Metro Levent.
An 800-seat concert hall with a prestigious programme and an unconventional location: in the basement of the highest skyscraper in Levent. Classical music concerts are performed by Turkish and foreign symphony and chamber orchestras. Other draws include recitals, jazz and world music.

Lütfi Kırdar Convention & Exhibition Centre
Lütfi Kırdar Kongre ve Sergi Sarayı

Darülbedayi Caddesi 60, Harbiye (0212 373 1100, www.icec.org/en). Bus 43, 46Ç, 46ÇY, 46H, 46KY.

The convention centre houses one of the city's biggest auditoriums, seating up to 3,500 people. Although it's not a dedicated music venue, it's actually one of Istanbul's top venues for classical music, along with the AKM.

Bosphorus Shore

Running along the banks of one of the world's busiest waterways, a chain of waterfront parks, palaces, and *yalıs* – 19th-century houses with lace-like trim – stretches from the Galata Bridge (see p72) and Karaköy (see p115) as far as the fortress and area of **Rumeli Hisarı**.

Along the way, the grandiose **Dolmabahçe Palace** dominates the busy waterfront at **Beşiktaş**, not far from the extensive grounds of **Yıldız Palace**. Further along, affluent **Ortaköy** and **Bebek** are known for their waterside cafés, restaurants and exclusive clubs.

Sights & museums

Dolmabahçe Palace
Dolmabahçe Sarayı
Dolmabahçe Caddesi (0212 236 9000). **Open** *May-Oct* 9am-4pm Tue, Wed, Fri-Sun. *Nov-Apr* 9am-3pm Tue, Wed, Fri-Sun. **Admission** YTL15. **Harem** YTL10.
Irrefutable evidence of an empire on its last legs, Dolmabahçe Palace was built for Abdül Mecit. It was completed in 1855, whereupon the sultan and his household moved in, abandoning Topkapı Palace. The outside is overwrought enough – though the façade of white marble is striking when viewed from the water – but it's trumped by the interior, the work of French decorator Sechan, who worked on the Paris Opera. 'Highlights' are the 36m-high throne room with its four-ton crystal chandelier (a gift from Queen Victoria), the alabaster baths, and a 'crystal staircase'. As it's still used for state functions, visits are in guided groups.

The former imperial kitchens house the Depot Museum (9am-5pm Tue-Sun, YTL2), a rambling collection of pieces salvaged from Dolmabahçe Palace's storage rooms: everything from samovars to Japanese porcelain.

Mimar Sinan University Museum of Fine Arts
Mimar Sinan Üniversitesi Istanbul Resim ve Heykel Müzesi
Barbaros Hayrettin Paşa Iskelesi Sokak, off Beşiktaş Caddesi (0212 261 4299). Bus 25E, 28, 40, 56. **Open** 10am-4.30pm Mon-Fri. **Admission** free.
The decrepit state of this poorly signposted museum, housed in a waterside mansion, suggests that few visitors find their way here. Shame, because the collection of Turkish art on display in the high-ceilinged halls includes some fine pieces. It all dates from the mid 19th to mid 20th century, and is mostly Orientalist in style.

Naval Museum
Deniz Müzesi
Barbaros Hayrettin Paşa Iskelesi Sokak, off Beşiktaş Caddesi (0212 327 4345). Bus 25E, 28, 40, 56. **Open** 9am-5pm Wed-Sun. **Admission** YTL4. No credit cards.
An extensive collection of model ships, mastheads and oil paintings, along with plenty of booty captured from British and French warships sunk during the abortive Dardanelles campaign of World War I. You'll also find the battle flag of Barbarossa, the notorious 16th-century pirate, and just about everything that wasn't nailed down on Atatürk's yacht, the *Savarona*. A smaller building houses an impressive collection of Ottoman caiques, elegant vessels that were as symbolic of the city as the gondola is to Venice.

Rumeli Hisarı Fortress
Rumeli Hisarı Müzesi
Yahya Kemal Caddesi (0212 263 5305). Bus 25E, 40. **Open** 9am-4.30pm daily. **Admission** YTL2. No credit cards.

Rumeli Hisarı

Consisting of three huge towers joined by crenellated defensive walls, the fortress was raised in a hurry as part of Mehmet II's master plan to capture Constantinople. Facing the 14th-century castle of Anadolu Hisarı (already in Ottoman hands) across the Bosphorus' narrowest stretch, Rumeli Hisarı was designed to cut maritime supply lines and isolate Constantinople from its allies. Designed by the sultan himself, work was completed in August 1452, just four months after it commenced. Garrisoned by Janissaries and bristling with cannon, Rumeli Hisarı proved its effectiveness immediately: a Venetian merchant vessel that attempted to run the blockade was promptly sunk.

Sakıp Sabancı Museum

Istinye Caddesi 22, Emirgan (0212 277 2200, http://muze.sabanciuniv.edu). Bus 22, 22RV, 25E. **Open** 10am-6pm Tue-Sun; 10am-10pmWed. **Admission** YTL10; YTL3 reductions.

Owned by one of Turkey's wealthiest businessmen, this museum is housed in a fabulous villa, built for Egyptian royalty in the 1920s on the shores of the Bosphorus. The steeply sloping lawns are scattered with stone treasures on loan from the Archaeology Museum.

Inside are two floors of exceptionally fine ceramics. It's particularly strong on Ottoman calligraphy and illumination. A modern extension holds a collection of 19th- and 20th-century Turkish art that unfortunately fails to do justice to its coolly elegant surroundings: the paintings also play second fiddle to the panoramic views.

Yıldız Chalet Museum

Yıldız Şale Müzesi

Palanga Caddesi 23, Yıldız Parkı (0212 259 8977). Bus 25E, 28, 40, 56. **Open** 9am-5pm Tue, Wed, Fri-Sun. **Admission** YTL4 Tue, Wed; YTL2 Fri-Sun. No credit cards.

The obligatory tour of this imperial pavilion takes you down dark, musty corridors leading to 60 rooms furnished with ornate furniture. The Grand Salon, a massive court chamber, now stands empty but for a line of chairs that highlight the sense of lost grandeur.

Yıldız Palace

Yıldız Sarayı

Yıldız Caddesi (0212 258 3080). Bus 25E, 28, 40, 56. **Open** 9am-4pm Tue-Sun. **Admission** YTL2. No credit cards.

Most of the palace dates from the late 19th century, when the paranoid Sultan Abdül Hamit II abandoned waterfront Dolmabahçe for fear of attack by foreign warships. The sultan was so fearful for his safety that no architect was allowed to see the complete plans for the new palace. Only the sultan knew the location of all the secret passages. The rooms open to visitors contain porcelain, furniture and some of Abdül Hamit's possessions.

Eating & drinking

Anjelique

Salhane Sokak 5, off Muallim Naci Caddesi, , Ortaköy (0212 327 2844). **Open** 6pm-4am daily. **Asian/ Mediterranean/Bar**.

This upmarket restaurant serving Asian and Mediterranean dishes turns into a club and cocktail bar later on. In a restored three-storey mansion, it has superb views over the Bosphorus. The music policy is key, and it even has its own *Sounds of Angelique* CD volumes. Big-name DJs regularly attend.

Aşşk Café

Muallim Naci Caddesi 64/B, Kuruçeşme (0212 265 4734). Bus 25E, 40T. **Open** 9am-2am Tue-Sun; noon-2am Mon. **Café (licensed)**.

This place has a lot to recommend it. To find it, follow the unmarked staircase down to the Bosphorus from the Macrocenter in Kuruçeşme. The setting is gorgeous: a clubhouse beside the Bosphorus with a lovely garden. The lavish breakfasts and organic salads are renowned, but rather overpriced.

Banyan Ortaköy

Muallim Naci Caddesi Salhane Sokak 3, Ortaköy (0212 259 9060, www.banyanrestaurant.com). Bus 40, 40T, 42T. **Open** noon-2am daily. **$$$**. **Asian**.

With spectacular views of the original Bosphorus bridge and floodlit Ortaköy mosque, Banyan is lovely on summer nights. Living up to the slogan 'Food for the Soul', all ingredients are organic and ethically sourced. The menu is a mix of Asian influences. Chinese, Japanese, Vietnamese and Indian delicacies are beautifully presented and prepared. This is fusion food at its best – good for the soul, but hard on the wallet.

House Café

Salhane Sokak 1, off Muallim Naci Caddesi, Ortaköy (0212 227 2699, www.thehousecafe.com.tr). Bus 40, 40T, 42T. **Open** 9am-2am Mon-Thur, Sun; 8am-2am Fri, Sat. **$$**. **Modern European**.

The House Café group's expansion could be called a phenomenon (see box p84). With industrial-chic interiors, all the locations offer lovely surroundings in which to enjoy a mishmash of global comfort food made with gourmet ingredients, but this Ortaköy café also has a blissful terrace right on the Bosphorus. Weekend brunch is a fixture for the young and well-heeled. Try the superlative House burger, thin-crust pizzas, imaginative bruschetta and salads. Fresh fruit cocktails are a joy to behold.

Mangerie

Cevdetpaşa Caddesi 69, Bebek (0212 263 5199, www.mangeriebebek.com). Bus 40, 40T, 42T. **Open** 8am-midnight daily. **$$**. **Modern Turkish**.

Tucked away behind the fancy waterside eateries in Bebek, this delightful restaurant is worth seeking out. (Head for the Küçük Bebek end of the high street and follow the steps leading up past a hairdresser.) The airy interior is all white wood, with a balcony that looks over the rooftops to the

Çiya

Remembered flavours.

It has been said that the food at **Çiya** (Güneşlibahçe Sokak 43-44, Kadıköy, 0216 418 5115, www.ciya.com.tr) can make people cry. The hint of a long-forgotten herb, or a lost Anatolian recipe, is to some what madeleines were to Proust.

Although it has expanded to three locations along the same street in Kadıköy, each with a slightly different focus, Çiya's quality remains the same. The original was launched in 1978 by Musa Dağdeviren, whose mission was to 'create an experimental cuisine with Anatolian food culture, which was losing power against fast food'. It is his years of research that informs the menu. Although defined as south-eastern and eastern Mediterranean, the influence of Azerbaijani, Georgian, Turkish, Arabic, Armenian, Ottoman, Syrian and Jewish food can all be discerned.

When he travels, Dağdeviren collects obscure ingredients, some of which make up the 1,000 or so dishes he'll put on the menu over a year. The restaurants themselves are unassuming. Çiya Sofrası specialises in traditional dishes from around Turkey. Opposite is Çiya Kebapçı, heaven for kebab aficionados.

Starters are buffet style. For mains, try the stuffed artichoke, meatballs, a stuffed intestine stew or a bit of everything. Or just let the affable waiters choose for you.

Cruising the Bosphorus

Istanbul's finest day out.

For centuries, the narrow waterway that separates Europe and Asia and snakes through the city's heart was Istanbul's *raison d'être*. Consequently, Istanbul has always presented its best face to the Bosphorus. The twisting shoreline is punctuated by imperial palaces, diplomatic hideaways and gorgeous old Ottoman *yalıs* (waterfront mansions), all ageing gracefully. A cruise up the Bosphorus is one of the highlights of any visit to Istanbul.

Many visitors opt for organised cruises. The state-run ferry company (www.ido.com.tr) runs a six-hour cruise for YTL25. Ferries depart daily all year round from Eminönü's Boğaz Hattı dock, 100 metres east of the Galata Bridge. Buy your tickets at the window labelled Eminönü-Kavaklar Boğaziçi Özel Gezi Seferleri (Eminönü-Kavaklar Bosphorus Special Tourist Excursions). Cruises depart at 10.30am and 1.30pm. Arrive 30 minutes early for good seats.

From Eminönü, the first stop is Beşiktaş, near Dolmabahçe Palace. The ferry then tacks back and forth between the European and Asian shores, stopping at several Bosphorous villages along the way: notably Kanlıca, Yeniköy, Sarıyer, Rumeli Kavağı and Anadolu Kavağı. You can get off wherever you like, but you will have to make your own way onwards or back to Eminönü. Most first-timers stay on board until Anadolu Kavağı, where there's enough time for lunch at one of the village's many fish restaurants before reboarding the ferry, which then makes a beeline back to Beşiktaş and Eminönü, with no other stops en route.

Numerous private operators run shorter boat trips that typically only go halfway up the Bosphorus, as far as Rumeli Hisarı, where passengers have an hour for lunch before the boat returns to Eminönü. The cheapest way, however, is to hop on the commuter ferries that crisscross the strait. It costs YTL1.50 per journey and is much more flexible.

Bosphorus. The relaxed atmosphere makes this an ideal lunch spot, with simple salads and sandwiches served on great breads, all baked on the premises. The house special *zeytinyağı*, seasonal vegetables and fruits stewed in olive oil, is recommended.

Müzedechanga

Sakıp Sabancı Caddesi 22, Emirgan (0212 323 0901, www.changa-istanbul. com). Metro Levent, then bus EL1, EL2. **Open** 10.30am-1am Tue-Sun. **$$$. Turkish/Mediterranean**.

In the Sakıp Sabancı Museum in Emirgan, Müzedechanga is much more than a museum café. Try to come here for lunch if you're anywhere in the area. It's housed in a mansion remodelled with a modern mixture of glass, wood and steel. The terrace has amazing views across the manicured museum gardens to the water. The Turkish-Med menu, supervised by constant chef Peter Gordon of Sugar Club fame, is faultless and well priced for this quality. Highly recommended.

Poseidon

Küçük Bebek, Cevdet Paşa Caddesi 58, Bebek (0212 263 3823, www.poseidon fish.com). Bus 40, 40T, 42T. **Open** noon-midnight daily. **$$$. Seafood**.

A supremely stylish affair, Poseidon serves superior seafood at vertiginous prices. Sampling the meze menu will hike up the bill, but specialities such as stuffed calamari, marinated sea bass and fish croquettes are worth it. The deck has gorgeous views of Bebek bay.

Rumeli Iskele

Yahya Kemal Caddesi 1, Rumeli Hisarı (0212 263 2997). Bus 40, 40T, 42T. **Open** noon-2am daily. **$$. Seafood**.

Despite competition from newer, shinier seafood restaurants, this place is always packed. The best tables are on the waterfront deck, with a view of the hilltop castle of Anadolu Hisarı across the strait. The menu holds few

surprises – meze and Mediterranean fish – but the food is good. Service is unobtrusive and efficient.

Sedir

Mecidiye Köprüsü Sokak 16-18, Ortaköy (0212 327 9870). Bus DT1, DT2. **Open** 9.30am-midnight daily. **Café**.

In a converted house next door to Ortaköy mosque, Sedir is a laid-back choice for all-day dining or a coffee break. The decor is designed to feel like home, with sofas, old books and hand-painted walls. The split-level conservatory is especially inviting.

Shopping

Ortaköy Market

Ortaköy Quayside. **Open** Sat, Sun.

Istanbul's answer to London's Camden Market. Go for mounds of tacky jewellery and plentiful kitsch imported from India and Africa. You might also find the odd interesting antique, reproduction print or choice trinket.

Nightlife

Anjelique

Salhane Sokak 5, off Muallim Naci Caddesi, Ortaköy (0212 327 2844). Bus DT1, DT2. **Open** 6pm-4am Mon-Sat.

The most tasteful of the Bosphorus bunch. Anjelique's assets include stunning views, above average food at the refined Da Mario restaurant, and delicious apple martinis. There are resident and excellent guest DJs, but Western and Turkish sing-along pap predominates.

Reina

Muallim Naci Caddesi 44, Ortaköy (0212 259 5919, www.reina.com.tr). Bus DT1, DT2. **Open** 7pm-4am daily.

The city's most famous nightclub, Reina is a stunning waterfront venue, resembling a swanky food court with a big dancefloor in the middle, hosting rich brats, celebs and wannabes. The music is pure Euro Med trash, and loud.

ISTANBUL BY AREA

World Class

Perfect places to stay, eat and explore.

Essentials

Tomtom Suites p145

Hotels

When it comes to deciding where to stay in Istanbul, there is basically one choice: south or north of the Golden Horn.

Most tourists who are visiting for a couple of days will head to one of the many hotels in **Sultanahmet** to be near the the Grand Bazaar and Topkapı Palace. This has traditionally been the centre for the city's budget accommodation. Many hotels in Sultanahmet have rooftop terraces and it's hard to beat morning coffee and croissants between the domes of the Haghia Sophia and Blue Mosque.

To be near the best bars and restaurants, find a hotel in **Beyoğlu**. More and more immaculately renovated mansions here have been imaginatively decorated and kitted out with the latest technology. Architects Autoban are behind the effortlessly stylish **Witt Istanbul** in Cihangir, as well as **House**

Hotel, which joins **Tomtom Suites** in neighbouring Çukurcuma.

Some classics have also received a facelift, including Istanbul's most famous hotel, the **Pera Palace Hotel**, whose guest book includes Greta Garbo and Jackie O. Further along Meşrutiyet Caddesi, the new **Mia Pera** hides a contemporary interior behind its 19th-century façade.

Most of the city's high-rise, high-end options for business travellers are clustered around Harbiye, an area of green parkland just north of Taksim Square. There's another cluster of hotels around the business district of 4. Levent, including the **Mövenpick**.

Information & prices

The price symbols in this chapter refer to the rack rates for standard double rooms. Prices can fluctuate wildly across the city and even in a single property. Tax and breakfast are usually included in the price.

Outside high season (late May to early September, and around Christmas) you can expect a discount of between 10 and 30 per cent. Hotels in the mid-range and budget categories are particularly open to bargaining over rates, especially if you're willing to pay your bill in cash in foreign currency.

Most places quote rates in euros but may accept dollars or sterling. Most take credit cards but may add a five to ten per cent surcharge.

Plenty of hotels take bookings online, and there are also a few useful websites for reservations, notably www.istanbulhotels.com, which brings together about 80 of the city's hotels. Or visit www.istanbul.hotelguide.net for links to local hotel websites.

There are several booking agents at Atatürk Airport in international arrivals (at the opposite end to the tourist information desk). They have an extensive list of mainly three- and four-star hotels and don't charge any commission.

South of the Golden Horn

Sultanahmet

Armada

Ahırkapı Sokak 24, Cankurtaran (0212 455 4455, www.armadahotel.com.tr). Cankurtaran rail. **$$.**
Sandwiched between waterside Kennedy Caddesi and the suburban railway line, the Armada scores low on location, although it is only a ten-minute walk to the sight-studded heart of Sultanahmet. The real advantage is that most rooms have fantastic, uninterrupted Bosphorus views. Modelled on a row of 19th-century houses that once stood here, the building is now a

SHORTLIST

Best new
- The House Hotel (see p145)
- Tomtom Suites (see p145)
- Witt Istanbul (see p146)

For Ottoman opulence
- Çırağan Palace Hotel Kempinski (see p148)
- Hotel les Ottomans (see p148)

For designer stays
- Mia Pera (see p142)
- Sofa Hotel (see p147)
- W Istanbul (see p149

Best budget stays
- Hotel Hanedan (see p138)
- Nomade Hotel (see p139)

Sultanahmet style
- Four Seasons (see p138)
- Eresin Crown Hotel (see p146)
- Yeşil Ev (see p140)

Best for food
- Richmond Hotel (see p142)
- Park Hyatt Maçka Palas (see p147)

Hotels with heritage
- Büyük Londra Hotel (see p141)
- Pera Palace (see p142)

Small but beautiful
- 5 oda (see p140)
- Eklektik Guest House (see p141)
- I'zaz Lofts (see p142)

Business class
- Ceylan Inter-Continental (see p142)
- Marmara Taksim (see p143)
- Mövenpick (see p147)

Best for backpackers
- Orient Hostel (see p139)
- Sultan Tourist Hostel (see p140)

ESSENTIALS

bit stuck in the 1980s. The fancy lobby has a terrapin pond and café, while the 110 rooms, if not exceptional, are certainly comfortable and slightly bigger than the average Sultanahmet room.

Ayasofya Pansiyonları

Soğukçeşme Sokak (0212 513 3660, www.ayasofyapensions.com). Tram Gülhane. **$$.**

In the 1980s, the Turkish Touring and Automobile Association reconstructed this row of nine clapboard houses dating from the 19th century. They were painted in pastel colours and furnished in period style. Rooms are all painted different colours and most have big brass beds. The setting is a dream: a sloping cobbled lane hidden between the high walls of Topkapı Palace and the back of Haghia Sophia. Breakfast is served in the pretty garden or the gazebo of the Konut Evi, a four-storey annexe at the end of the alley. At night, the whole place is lamp-lit. Walt Disney couldn't have created more magic.

Citadel

Kennedy Caddesi Sahilyolu 32, Ahır Kapı Sokak (0212 516 2313, www.citadelhotel.com). Cankurtaran rail. **$$.**

Occupying a striking pink three-storey mansion, this Best Western affiliate has 25 rooms and six suites decked out in Barbie colours. The only thing between you and the Sea of Marmara is – alas – six lanes of speeding traffic. It's not far from the fish restaurants of Kumkapı, though, and the conservatory bar and decent restaurant lessen the feeling of isolation. Free airport pick-ups.

Dersaadet

Kuçük Ayasofya Caddesi Kapıağası Sokak 5 (0212 458 0760, www.hotel dersaadet.com). Tram Sultanahmet. **$$.**

The Dersaadet (one of the many former names for Istanbul) has become one of the most popular boutique hotels south of the Golden Horn. Its quaint wooden

exterior and 19th-century French-influenced Ottoman decor recreate the charms of the Ottoman golden years. The 17 rooms, across four floors, are all comfortable, and some have good views over the Sea of Marmara. There is a pleasant rooftop breakfast terrace, with both indoor and outdoor tables, overlooking the Bosphorus and superb for enjoying an afternoon coffee to the sound of classical music. It's a non-smoking hotel.

Empress Zoe

Adliye Sokak 10, off Akbıyık Caddesi (0212 518 2504, www.emzoe.com). Tram Sultanahmet. **$$.**

Named after a racy Byzantine regent, the Zoe is one of the best and quirkiest of the city's small hotels. Its sunken reception area incorporates parts of a 15th-century hammam; the 'archaeological garden' is ideal for breakfast or a beer. Bear in mind that guests must be agile, as rooms are reached via a wrought-iron spiral staircase. In contrast to the gilt and frills of most other 'period' hotels, the Zoe's 19 small rooms are decorated in dark wood and richly coloured textiles. A new wing of suites has recently been added and the garden expanded. Add a fine rooftop bar for a nightcap with a view and this place is sheer class from top to bottom.

Eresin Crown Hotel

Küçük Ayasofya Caddesi 40 (0212 638 4428, www.eresincrown.com.tr). Tram Sultanahmet. **$$$.**

The Eresin Crown is unusual as a medium-sized, high-end hotel amid small 'Ottoman' boutique competitors in Sultanahmet: it's on the southern side of the peninsula, a stone's throw from Sultanahmet Mosque. Decor in the public spaces is pretty standard, of the marble and plate glass variety, but the hotel's unique selling point are the 50 or so artefacts discovered when the hotel was being built. Some rooms are on the small side, but all are comfortable and well appointed, with jacuzzis; there are

Bed, board and legends

One of the world's most famous hotels is back in business.

Built in 1892 as the last stop on the Orient Express, the **Pera Palace Hotel** (p142) is the most aristocratic of hotels. The same company that ran the famed Paris to Istanbul trains built the hotel along similarly luxurious lines, and in the early days its pampered guests were carried on cushioned sedans from Sirkeci Station to waiting hotel transport. In later years, superseded in comfort and facilities by the modern, sleek and efficient five-stars, the Pera Palace ceased to be the preserve of the statesmen, stars and spies that used to cross its still well-polished and buffed lobby, site of one successful and one failed assassination attempt.

A rather tired Pera Palace closed for refurbishment in 2006. Four years and €23 million later, it has reopened as a 'museum hotel'.

Architects have sympathetically retained the original character of the building, designed by Istanbul resident Alexander Vallaury in neo-classical, art nouveau and oriental styles. The Murano glass chandeliers and white Carrara

marble remain in the suites, alongside Wi-Fi and flatscreen TVs.

Guests at the new Pera Palace will be in exalted company. King Edward VIII, Queen Elizabeth II, Emperor Franz Joseph, Zsa Zsa Gabor, Sarah Bernhardt, Alfred Hitchcock, Pierre Loti and Jacqueline Kennedy Onassis have all laid their heads on the fluffy pillows. Agatha Christie was one of the most renowned guests. She wrote part of *Murder on the Orient Express* in room 411, which has been restored to be exactly as it was when she stayed here.

The Atatürk Museum Room (no.101) can only been visited, not slept in. Personal belongings and a range of items from the early days of the republic are here.

The Pera's new restaurant is called the Agatha (what else?). The Patisserie de Pera is a fine little Viennese-style coffee shop, while the bar is the place to enjoy a cocktail while musing upon the decline of servile porters, silk-stocking glamour and lobby shoot-outs, all rarities in the hotels of today.

several suites. The Terrace Restaurant has amazing views over the city, the Bosphorus and Sea of Marmara.

Four Seasons

Tevkifhane Sokak 1 (0212 638 8200, www.fourseasons.com/istanbul). Tram Sultanahmet. **$$$$.**

For 66 years this distinctive building, with its ochre walls and watchtowers, served as the infamous Sultanahmet Prison; inmates included celebrated political prisoners. Sensitively renovated in 1986, the Four Seasons has held on to its position as one of Istanbul's best hotels. With its manicured gardens and elegant gazebo restaurant (Seasons, see p62), the former prison yard has been transformed into an oasis of calm in the heart of bustling Sultanahmet. Cells have been replaced by 65 plush, high-ceilinged rooms and suites – a modest number that ensures intimacy and superlative service.

Hanedan

Adliye Sokak 3, Akbıyk Caddesi (0212 516 4869, www.hanedanhotel.com). Tram Sultanahmet. **$.**

Hanedan is one of the smartest independent hotels south of the Four Seasons. Clean, bright primrose-yellow rooms, with large beds draped in muslin, all have ensuite bathrooms with hairdryers and heated towel rails. The three family rooms have the best Marmara views. There are more unobstructed views from the roof terrace. It can be noisy on summer nights, when neighbouring hotels often host late-night rooftop parties.

Hotel Ararat

Torun Sokak 3 (0212 516 0411, www.ararathotel.com). Tram Sultanahmet. **$.**

Ararat's best feature is probably its location. Envious of the success of the nearby Empress Zoe, the young Turkish owners of Ararat recruited the same architect, Nicos Papadakis, to revamp their 12-room guesthouse. If the results aren't quite as inspired, the Ararat still breaks the mould, with marbled walls and an orange and ochre colour scheme that works well with the dark, stained-wood floors. Rooms vary widely in terms of size and comfort – some are small with little light, while others have wooden four-posters with great views of Sultanahmet Mosque. Breakfast is served on the roof terrace.

Hotel Uyan

Utangaç Sokak 25 (0212 516 4892, www.uyanhotel.com). Tram Sultanahmet. **$$.**

This attractive corner hotel in a 75-year-old building has 16 spacious standard rooms and ten suites spead over four floors. The standard rooms are simply furnished, with small bathrooms. Deluxe suites have a jacuzzi and sound system in the bathroom. Uyan's main selling point is that it has the highest roof terrace in the neighbourhood, with views over the Sultanahmet Mosque. The hotel offers free airport pick-ups.

Ibrahim Paşa Hotel

Terzihane Sokak 5 (0212 518 0394, www.ibrahimpasha.com). Tram Sultanahmet. **$$.**

Tucked round the corner from the Museum of Turkish and Islamic Art, the Ibrahim Paşa is an eminently likeable small hotel. It doesn't overplay the old Ottoman card and instead is stylishly modern, smart and bright, with just enough judiciously placed artefacts (including some fascinating old photographs in the breakfast area) to remind you that this is Istanbul. Rooms can be small, but judicious use is made of space. Staff are helpful; the ambience calm and relaxed. There are plenty of minarets and domes on show from the rooftop terrace.

Kybele Hotel

Yerebatan Caddesi 33-35 (0212 511 7766, www.kybelehotel.com). Tram Sultanahmet. **$$.**

The Akbayrak brothers obviously have a thing about vintage glass lamps – the interior of their hotel is hung with 2,000 of them. The eccentricities continue: every room is crammed with kilims, candlestands, empty bottles and quirky knick-knacks. Garish pink and green paint schemes heighten the sense of fun. The 16 bedrooms are smallish, particularly the singles, but they are comfortable enough and all have fancy marble bathrooms. Breakfast is served in a courtyard as colourful as a gypsy caravan.

Nomade Hotel

15 Ticarethane Sokak (0212 513 8172, www.hotelnomade.com). Tram Sultanahmet. $.
The cosy reception area, with comfortable design-minded furnishing, is perfect for watching the bustling pedestrian traffic outside, while the cushion-strewn, flower-filled roof terrace is one of the prettiest in Istanbul, particularly at night. The hotel's new owners refurbished the 16 rooms and reception area in 2010. The rooms are as cosy and uncluttered as before, with pastel walls, ethnic bedspreads, richly hued wall hangings and modern bathrooms.

Orient Hostel

Akbıyık Caddesi 13 (0212 518 0789, www.orienthostel.com). Tram Sultanahmet. $.
For years the Orient has been one of the mainstays of the Istanbul backpacker scene. Besides the full range of budget traveller services, including cheap internet access, money-changing facilities and discounted airline tickets, the Orient has a lively social scene, with barbecues, belly-dancing and film nights. There is also a women-only dormitory. Both this hostel and the Sultan (see p140) can fill up with local high school students during holiday time, or school groups from further afield.

St Sophia

Alemdar Caddesi 2 (0212 528 0973, www.saintsophiahotel.com). Tram Gülhane. $.
In the shadow of the Haghia Sophia and across the road from the Yerebatan Sarnıcı, this Best Western affiliate is yet another conversion of a 19th-century house. Extensive renovations have left it a bit over-polished and lacking in atmosphere. The 27 rooms have modern furnishings; those on the top two floors have jacuzzis and balconies that overlook Justinian's great cathedral.

Sarnıç

Küçük Ayasofya Caddesi 26 (0212 518 2323, www.sarnichotel.com). Tram Sultanahmet. $$.
Sarnıç, the Turkish word for cistern, takes its name from the fifth-century Byzantine cistern beneath the hotel, which guests can explore from 9am to 6pm. After changing ownership, Sarnıç underwent major renovations in 2010. Another five rooms were added on the top floor – recommended for the views of Sultanahmet Mosque. Other rooms have been tastefully decorated, and include flatscreen TVs. The small top-floor terrace is particularly scenic at sunset, and there's a bar/breakfast room below ground. Popular half-day cookery courses take place in the hotel kitchen. The hotel is only a few minutes' walk from the Hippodrome.

Side Hotel & Pension

Utangaç Sokak 20 (0212 517 2282, www.sidehotel.com). Tram Sultanahmet. $. No credit cards.
Rooms are clean and well looked after here, and have ensuite bathrooms with shower cubicles (the Istanbul norm for this price bracket is a shower that falls straight on to the bathroom floor). Rooms vary widely, so ask to look at a few before you make your choice. Pension accommodation is more basic; the cheapest room has a shared but clean bathroom. There are two self-catering appartments for large groups.

Eklektik Guest House

Breakfast is served on the rooftop terrace. There's free tea available in the rustic, wood-panelled foyer and a small book exchange.

Sultan Tourist Hostel

Terbıyık Sokak 3, off Akbıyık Caddesi (0212 516 9260, www.sultanhostel. com). Tram Sultanahmet. **$**.

Another backpacker staple, virtually next door to the Orient, the Sultan has bright and airy singles, doubles and mixed-sex dormitories, although having only a single shower/toilet on each floor is a major drawback. There's a restaurant up top, as well as a bar, pub, disco, games room with table tennis and darts, and computer centre. The Sultan Café on the street is a good place for a beer.

Turkoman

Asmalıçeşme Sokak 2, off the Hippodrome (0212 516 2956, www.turkomanhotel.com). Tram Sultanahmet. **$**.

Located just off the Hippodrome and opposite the Egyptian obelisk, the Turkoman's roof terrace has amazing views of the Sultanahmet Mosque, although in the summer the mosque is hidden from the lower floors by foliage. Bright, unfussy and very yellow rooms verge on the tacky, but have brass beds, parquet flooring and big windows. Free one-way airport transfer is available for guests staying more than three nights.

Yeşil Ev

Kabasakal Caddesi 5 (0212 517 6785, www.istanbulyesilev.com). Tram Sultanahmet. **$$$**.

Flagship of the Turkish Touring and Automobile Association's fleet of restored Ottoman properties, the 'Green House' enjoys an unrivalled location on a leafy street midway between the Haghia Sophia and Sultanahmet Mosque. Entering this stately wooden mansion is like stepping on to the set of a 19th-century costume drama. Every room is decked out in reproduction furniture, complete with wood-panelled ceilings, creaky parquet flooring and antique rugs. The Sultan's Suite has its own hammam. The idyllic garden is one of the highlights, with a pretty pink pond, a fine café and beer garden and the restaurant. With only 19 rooms, booking in advance is essential.

Beyazıt

Hotel Niles

Ordu Caddesi Dibekli, Cami Sokak 19 (0212 517 3239, www.hotelniles.com). Tram Beyazıt. **$$**.

Significantly refurbished in 2010, Hotel Niles is owned by the same family that is responsible for the highly regarded Dersaadet. They have been involved in every detail of the renovations, from the authentic Iznik tiles to the design on the hand-painted ceiling. Each of the ten new suites is based on French-influenced Ottoman style, done out in light turquoise. They're equipped with microwaves and have hammam-style bathrooms with Marmara marble. There's a gym, conference room and leafy roof garden, where breakfast is served. Service is flawless.

Beyoğlu

Galata & Tünel

5 oda

Şahkulu Bostan Sokak 164 (0212 252 7501, www.5oda.com). **$$**.

This new guesthouse, on a quiet street just off Istiklal Caddesi, is perfectly located for the bars and shopping of Beyoğlu. The five rooms are accessed through a reception/kitchen area, and a small glass-sided elevator. They are long and airy, with large windows at either side. The architect has used the space well, with an open-plan design that includes a kitchen area with sink, hob, fridge and coffee-making facilities, a couple of chairs and a glass table. With modern design, using wood and white-painted bare brickwork, they are relaxing spaces. Bathrooms are small, with only enough room for a shower, basin and toilet. Breakfasts, which can be served in the room, are excellent.

Eklektik Guest House

Kadribey Cikmazi 4 (0212 243 7446, www.eklektikgalata.com). **$$**. No credit cards.

This thoroughly charming guesthouse, on a quiet cul-de-sac, is popular with gay visitors, but the friendly and knowledgeable staff make everyone feel very welcome. Each of the eight smallish rooms is decorated to a theme: from clean lines, white walls and wood in the Zen Room to drapes and ornate lamps in the Colonial Room, and black linens – and a mirror ball in the bathroom – in the Black Room. Downstairs is the new Hammam Room, with heated floors and a Marmara marble bathing area. The shower in the corner of most rooms is an unconventional touch, but it doesn't seem to bother the patrons, and nor does the lack of a lift. There is a small terrace with views over the Bosphorus. The breakfast, served around one large table, is superb.

Galata Residence

Felek Sokak 27, off Bankalar Caddesi (0212 292 4841, www.galataresidence.com). **$**.

An apartment hotel with history. The house formerly belonged to the Kamondos, an important Levantine banking family, who gave their name to the sculpted steps that lead up to the residence from Voyvoda Caddesi. The solid brick building later served as a Jewish school. It is now split into 15 comfortably furnished apartments, which each sleep four. Smaller two-bedroom apartments are available in the next building. The decor is homely and old-fashioned, with four-poster beds, vintage armchairs and sofas. Each apartment has a fully equipped kitchen, but there's also a restaurant on the roof and a bare-brick café in the vaulted cellar. It is close enough to walk across the bridge to Eminönü and the bazaar, but just downhill from the Galata Tower and Beyoğlu.

Pera

Büyük Londra Hotel

Meşrutiyet Caddesi 53 (0212 245 0670, www.londrahotel.net). **$**.

The Londra was built in 1892, so it's roughly the same age as the nearby Pera Palace Hotel. But where the Pera Palace is grand, the Londra is homely and eccentric. Caged parrots peer dolefully from their cages on the windowsills in the lounge-bar (see p90). Portable coal burners, wind-up gramophones, valve radios and plenty of other ancient junk clutter the corridors. Hemingway stayed here in 1922, sent by the *Toronto Daily Star* to cover the Turkish war of independence, and the place is still favoured by artists, writers and film crews. Some of the 54 rooms are a little on the down-at-heel side, but they are clean. The upper floors have 'super' rooms with double glazing, plush carpets and jacuzzis.

Mia Pera
Meşrutiyet Caddesi 53 (0212 245 0245, www.miaperahotel.com). **$$$.**
One of the latest additions to Beyoğlu's burgeoning hotel scene is also one of the most stylish. Only the façade of this 19th-century French style Ottoman residence remains intact. Once through the glass doors, Mia Pera is a thoroughly modern experience. Copies of *Wallpaper** magazines are stacked next to coloured glass vases on the shelves in the lobby. Down three steps are the bar, restaurant and breakfast room (the breakfast buffet is excellent here). The single rooms are on the small side, but thoughtful design makes the best use of the space available. Deluxe rooms are significantly larger and there are also four duplex suites. The highlight, however, is the basement spa and heated oval pool – a relaxing and warming hammam-style affair. Massages are available.

Pera Palace Hotel
Meşrutiyet Caddesi 98 (0212 251 4560, www.perapalace.com). **$$$$.** See box p137.

Istiklal Caddesi

Residence
Sadri Alışık Sokak 19, off Istiklal Caddesi (0212 252 7685, www. hotelresidence.com.tr). **$.**
The Residence is a bit difficult to find as it's tucked away on a narrow side street, but it's worth the effort. The rooms, though small and basic, are bright and well equipped, and recently refurbished. The location is great too, right among the bars of Beyoğlu.

Richmond Hotel
Istiklal Caddesi 227 (0212 252 5460, www.richmondhotels.com.tr). **$$$.**
The Richmond is the best hotel on Istiklal Caddesi, Beyoğlu's main thoroughfare. This always busy pedestrianised street, lined with shops, cafés, bars and plenty of grand old apartment blocks ripe for conversion, has been oddly overlooked by hotel developers. The Richmond has retained the building's historic façade, but the interior has been ripped out, and rooms are undergoing a second renovation in 2010. What the interior lacks in style, the hotel makes up for with a relaxed atmosphere and friendly staff. Standard rooms are simple and streamlined, while the executive suites cater mainly to business travellers. The sleek Leb-i Derya bar-restaurant (see p96) probably has the best view of any of Istanbul's rooftop bars.

Nevizade

I'zaz Lofts
Balik Sokak 12 (212 252 1382, www.izaz.com). **$$.**
There are only four ('lofts') at I'zaz, each replete with considered design touches. They're well appointed, with large beds, a desk, flatscreen TV, iPod dock and coffee-making facilities. Visitors should bear in mind that the upper rooms can only be accessed by a staircase. The location is excellent for the bars and restaurants of Nevizade

(the hotel entrance is on a nondescript street, just out of earshot of the action). There's a lovely seating area with vast views over the minarets of Kasımpaşa and the western side of the city. I'zaz's hands-off philosophy means it can feel more like an apartment outfit than a hotel: if they want to, guests can cook for themselves in the communal kitchen (where there's always a pot of coffee on the go) or do their own laundry. But staff are also on hand and can cater to most whims.

Taksim

Ceylan Inter-Continental

Asker Ocağı Caddesi 1 (0212 368 4444, www.istanbulintercontinental.com.tr). **$$$**.
The Inter-Continental is an 18-floor Goliath. Renovated in 2008, the style remains brash, the tone set by a golden staircase spiralling up from the lobby and a glitzy, palm-filled atrium. Decor aside, the hotel is well appointed, although most of the rooms are a bit smaller than others in this price range. Those on the Club Floor (actually the top four floors) are better, but pricey. The Safran restaurant was recommended

by Acàdemie Internationale de la Gastronomie and top-floor City Lights bar offers spectacular views but steep prices. The hotel is a ten-minute walk from central Taksim Square.

Madison Hotel

Recep Paşa Caddesi 15 (0212 238 5460, www.themadisonhotel.com.tr). **$$**.
North-west of Taksim Square, between Tarlabaşı Bulvarı and Cumhuriyet Caddesi, are a series of quiet streets that are home to a number of reasonable mid-range hotels, including this one. The Madison is a modern four-star place with decent-sized rooms. Insipid colour scheme aside, there's little cause for complaint. Bathrooms are small but clean and practical, decked out in marble. All the rooms were renovated in 2010. The indoor poolside bar is a relaxed place to hang out.

Marmara Taksim

Taksim Square (0212 251 4696, www.themarmarahotels.com). **$$$**.
One of four Marmara hotels in Istanbul (with sister establishments in Manhattan and across Turkey), this location is a Taksim Square landmark. It is the place to stay if you want to be

Witt p146

Design for life

Istanbul's new take on style hotels.

It's no exaggeration to say that Istanbul's design culture is burgeoning. So much so that the city is developing its own style, melding 19th-century Ottoman opulence with a mid-century-modern aesthetic. For the last decade, bars and restaurants have excelled in fabulous retro design. Now hotels are catching up.

Two of the newest additions to Istanbul's hotel scene are the **Witt Istanbul** (see p146) and the **House Hotel** (see right) in Çukurcuma, both genuinely impressive.

Also around Çukurcuma is **Tomtom Suites** (see p145), which has immaculately designed details – from the light switches to the bedlinen to the art on the walls.

Always keen to ride the zeitgeist is the Starwood **W** hotel group. Its new hotel (see p149) is apparently based on an Ottoman jewellery box. It's certainly glitzy, perfect for DJ nights, fashion shows and other such events.

Another corporate offering, the **Park Hyatt Maçka Palas** (see p147), is Istanbul's most surprising new hotel, with ergonomic desks, the latest gadgetry and steam rooms.

Our favourite true boutique hotels that emphasise design are **I'zaz Lofts** (see p142), **5 oda** (see p141) and **Eklektik Guest House** (see p141), all in Beyoğlu.

at the heart of the action, though bear in mind that Taksim Square is far from picturesque. The hotel isn't quite as polished as its international rivals, and the 448 rooms have the facilities and feel of a big chain hotel. Most have decent views, but the best lookout spot is from the top-floor Tepe Lounge or the Panorama restaurant.

Taksim Square Hotel

Sıraselviler Caddesi 15, Taksim Square (0212 292 6440, www.taksimsquare hotel.com.tr). **$$**.

Right in the centre of town, this modern, high-rise hotel is modestly priced but lacks charm. Just 32 of the 87 rooms have a view across the rooftops to the Bosphorus; in the rest, guests have to be content with looking down on the street life on busy Sıraselviler and the diners on the rooftop terrace of Burger King opposite.

Taksim Suites

Cumhuriyet Caddesi 49 (0212 254 7777, www.taximsuites.com). **$$**.

These self-catering suites make an ideal base for business people. The Miyako suites take their inspiration from the east, while the Park and Avenue suites look towards Scandinavia. Fully equipped with everything from microwaves to fax machines, the five options range from a 45sq m (480sq ft) studio to a 109sq m (1,150 sq ft) penthouse with remote-controlled skylights and Bosphorus views. Additional treats include breakfast in bed (or the Taksim Lounge), jacuzzis, a fitness room, wireless internet, and accommodating staff who will buy your groceries if you leave a shopping list at reception. Another plus is the excellent location just minutes from Taksim Square.

Vardar Palace Hotel

Sıraselviler Caddesi 16 (0212 252 2888, www.vardarhotel.com). **$**.

Two minutes from Taksim Square, the 40-room Vardar occupies a drab-looking 19th-century building on a narrow

Park Hyatt Maçka Palas p147

strip, where Sıraselviler narrows to almost canyon-like proportions. Inside, however, the hotel is bright, pleasant and deserving of its three-star status, although the airiness of the high-ceilinged rooms is sabotaged by a dark colour scheme. Front-facing rooms can get noisy.

Çukurcuma

House Hotel
Firuzağa Mahallesi, Bostanbaşı Caddesi 19 (0212 252 0422, www.thehouse-hotels.com). **$$**.
This stunning new hotel is partly owned by the House Café group, and the same sensitive design aesthetic found in the cafés shines through here. It's located in a converted mansion built in 1850, on a quiet street in the Çukurcuma antique district. Going through the elegant but unassuming entrance, you'll find the original tiled floors and Italian marble staircase. Upstairs, each of the 20 well-equipped suites has been designed with the neighbourhood in mind – the tiles in the bathrooms list traditional family names of the area. Decor is a subtly modern take on the traditional, with

mixed shades of wood adding pattern to parquet flooring, panelled walls painted white and sleek, updated chandeliers. Furnishings in dove grey add a slightly ethereal touch to the white. The bar, on the top floor (bear in mind there are no lifts), has Chesterfield sofas from which to admire views over the Galata Tower.

Tomtom Suites
Boğazkesen Caddesi, Tomtom Kaptan Sokak 18 (0212 292 4949, www.tomtomsuites.com). **$$$**.
It's the size of Tomtom Suites that's immediately striking. The standard rooms are 35-45sq m (376-484sq ft), and the senior suites 55-65sq m (582-700sq ft). The high ceilings of this converted Franciscan nunnery only add to the impressive proportions. The beds are enormous, and each room has a jacuzzi. Named for its road and nearby mosque, Tomtom Suites was restored and repurposed in 2008 with a modern classic design that has maintained original features such as the staircase. Modern artwork and a glass lift, which can be seen rising to the fourth floor, greet the visitor. The terrace restaurant and patio has panoramic views over the Golden Horn.

ESSENTIALS

Four Seasons Bosphorus p148

Cihangir

Villa Zurich

Akarsu Yokuşu Caddesi 36/36A (0212 293 0604, www.hotelvillazurich.com). **$**.
Ten minutes' walk down Sıraselviler Caddesi from Taksim Square, the Villa Zurich is conveniently close to the centre but pleasantly removed from all the hustle. The area itself is worth exploring – a lively mix of local shops and tea houses mixed with hip cafés and gourmet delis. The Villa Zurich is vaguely European in character, with 43 comfortable, if unremarkable, guest rooms and two suites. There is a popular seafood restaurant, Doğa Balık (see p112) on the rooftop, with fabulous views.

Witt Istanbul

Defterdar Yokusu, 26 (0212 293 1500, www.wittistanbul.com). **$$$**.
Designed by local company Autoban in a modern-meets-retro style, the Witt Istanbul is a deeply impressive suite hotel. Attention to detail is apparent everywhere: from the open-plan

arrangement of the suites to the staff uniforms. The lobby, bar and dining/breakfast areas are low lit, with only black tiles reflecting the light. Suites are spacious, and include a kitchenette. There is also a seating area, large beds and a desk with an iPod dock. Ross Lovegrove-designed marble bathrooms have showers with five showerheads and bespoke towels. Walls are soundproofed. Not all suites have a great view, so ask for one that does. The location is convenient for both the hip cafés along Akarsu Sokak and the antique shops of Çukurcuma.

Beyond the Centre
West

Kariye Hotel

Kariye Camii Sokak 6, Edirnekapı (0212 534 8414, www.kariyeotel.com). **$$**.
Another 19th-century Ottoman residence stripped down and dressed up by the Turkish Touring and Automobile Association. There are 26 rooms, all done out in early 1900s

fashion. There is also a family annexe with one master bedroom and a single room. The restaurant, Asitane (see p121), is renowned for its authentic Ottoman cuisine. Next door is the Church of St Saviour in Chora, one of Istanbul's essential sights. But the big snag is the location, out by the old city walls and about a half-hour bus ride from Sultanahmet, or around YTL10 in a taxi.

Polat Renaissance Istanbul Hotel

Sahil Yolu 2 Caddesi, Yeşilyurt (0212 414 1800, www.polatrenaissance.com). **$$$**.

Our airport hotel of choice, the Polat Renaissance is a five-minute taxi ride from the terminal in the coastal suburb of Yeşilköy (it's 18 kilometres, or 12 miles, from the city centre). A 27-storey blue glass skyscraper by the sea, with an ultra-modern interior that features a soaring central atrium. At least half the 414 rooms have views over the Marmara. All the rooms were renovated in 2010 and now have LCD TVs, broadband internet access and coffee machines. All the facilities you would expect of a Marriott hotel are present, including a large, heated outdoor pool.

North

Bentley Hotel

Halaskargazi Caddesi 23, Harbiye (0212 291 7730, www.bentley-hotel.com). **$$$$**.

Istanbul's first (self-proclaimed) 'hip' hotel, the Bentley's minimalist chocolate-and-cream lobby looks like the reception area of an upmarket ad agency. Rooms are similarly smart and understated. Best options are the corner rooms with curving glass walls (a pity there's not much of a view). The two penthouse suites have wine mini-bars, plasma TVs and espresso machines. One comes with an adjacent single room. These are stylish amenities, as you would expect from a member of the Design Hotels group, but there's nothing groundbreaking.

Mövenpick

Buyukdere Caddesi, 4. Levent (0212 319 2929, www.movenpick-hotels.com). **$$$**.

The pick of the hotels in corporate 4. Levent, the Swiss-owned Mövenpick is a good business option, but its location very near 4. Levent metro stop means it is hand for central Taksim square too. The 249 rooms are well designed, with plain wood and natural colours, and rooms on the higher floors have good views. For guests paying the executive rate, there's an airpor-style lounge on the 20th floor. Others have to make do with the chic Baradox lobby bar and lounge. The dimly lit and cavernous wellness centre has a gym, sauna, jacuzzi and swimming pool.

Park Hyatt Maçka Palas

Tesvikiye, Bronz Sokak 4 isli Şişli, Şişli (0212 315 1234, www.istanbul.park.hyatt.com). **$$$$**.

Leave your preconceptions of international chain hotels in the atrium lobby, this Park Hyatt in Şişli is one of a new generation of large hotels that are responding to the boutique phenomenon. The result is an impressive, converted from what used to be the Italian Embassy before the capital moved to Ankara. Each of the 90 rooms has plenty of space, with modern gadgets for the business traveller. Bathrooms have a steam room, which in cheaper rooms contains the shower. Some also have a hammam-style area with heated marble floors. Other nice touches include a filtered water sink, alongside a regular one, iPod docks and deep stand-alone baths. Photos from Ara Güler hang around the hotel. In the lobby is a wine lounge, but more impressive is the Terrace, with a small pool.

Sofa Hotel

Teşvikiye Caddesi 123, Nişantaşı (0212 368 1818, www.thesofahotel.com). **$$$$**.

The Sofa Hotel offers minimalist chic in the heart of Nişantaşı's upmarket shopping and dining area, and is also within walking distance of the Istanbul Convention and Exhibition Center. The design-led bedrooms are comfortable, and the well-equipped bathrooms feature rainshowers and fluffy bathrobes. There's a decent spa and fitness room, and the in-house restaurant, Longtable (see p123), serves modern New York cuisine in handsome surroundings.

Bosphorus Shore

Bebek Hotel

Cevdet Paşa Caddesi 34, Bebek (0212 358 2000, www.bebekhotel.com.tr). **$$$**.
Far from the centre and the sights, this is primarily a business hotel. From the outside, the four-storey building is nothing special, but inside the 21 suites are all gleaming dark wood, brown leather, pink marble and rattan furniture. The real wow factor here is the view, and nine of the rooms have balconies over the Bosphorus. Is it worth the extra €90? We'd have to say yes. However, if you get stuck with a room overlooking the street, you can enjoy the same view from the waterfront bar downstairs. Beware of Bebek in the summer, when the traffic into town can be agonisingly slow.

Çırağan Palace Hotel Kempinski

Çırağan Caddesi 32, Beşiktaş (0212 258 3377, www.kempinski.com). **$$$$**.
The hotel is partly set in a magnificent 19th-century palace on the Bosphorus built for Sultan Abdülaziz, an ill-fated ruler who killed himself with a pair of scissors. In 1908, the palace became the seat of parliament, but burned down two years later. In 1986, following an ambitious restoration, parts of the original complex were incorporated into this luxurious, 313-room extravaganza belonging to the Kempinski chain. Only 11 suites are in the palace itself – including the €30,000-a-night Sultan's

suite – along with the Tuğra restaurant, which showcases Ottoman cuisine, and other public rooms. All other bedrooms are in the annexe. Non-residents can enjoy the hotel's art and culture programme, which includes exhibitions. There are free classical concerts on the first and last Saturday of every month (call to reserve). In summer, take advantage of the stunning outdoor infinity pool, which appears to flow into the Bosphorus.

Four Seasons Bosphorus

Çırağan Caddesi 28, Beşiktaş (0212 381 4000, www.fourseasons.com/ bosphorus). **$$$$**.
The second Four Seasons property in Istanbul is a very different proposition from the Sultanahmet hotel. This one, near Kempinski's Çırağan Palace, is a 19th-century palace on the Bosphorus, looking over to the Asian shore. Its classic design will reassure those used to the Four Seasons brand, although there are Ottoman touches throughout, too. Rooms and suites all have a TV, DVD and CD player, and a deep marble bath. The grounds are delightful for taking a stroll before dinner to watch the ships roll past. If it's warm outside, the pool bar and terrace is the spot to take dinner.

Hotel les Ottomans

Muallim Naci Caddesi 168, Kuruçeşme (0212 287 1024, www.lesottomans.com). **$$$$**.
Opened in spring 2006, this all-suite hotel is designed to lure celebrities, heads of state and millionaires bored of the Çırağan Palace. In an impeccably restored white wooden *yalı* (mansion), with spectacular views of the Boğazici Strait, the style is Oriental opulence – to excess, some might say. Think brocade drapes, Arabic-script inscriptions and giant chandeliers. With just 12 suites, the emphasis is on exclusivity. Butler, yacht and limousine service are all part of the package. The Passionate Suite is, of course, billed as the perfect honeymoon destination – with feng

shui to 'add a completely new freshness and purity to your life as a couple'. There's an intimate Ottoman restaurant with an impressive cellar and a fabulous Caudalie spa.

Princess Hotel Ortaköy

Dereboyu Caddesi 10, Ortaköy (0212 227 6010, www.ortakoyprincess.com). **$$$**.

Few people other than those doing business up in nearby Levent and Maslak choose to stay in Ortaköy, but if scurrying around the mosques isn't on your agenda, this rather bland option is worth considering. A modern hotel with 90 generously sized rooms, its most appealing feature is probably its proximity to the waterfront bars, cafés and fish restaurants. You can avoid the traffic that clogs Istanbul's roads by catching a ferry down the Bosphorus to the sights in Sultanahmet.

W Istanbul

NEW *Suleyman Seba Caddesi 22, Akaretler, Beşiktaş (0212 381 2121, www.wistanbul.com.tr).* **$$$**.

The ultra-styled design of W hotels around the world continues with this new Beşiktaş property. The hotel is in a recently redeveloped area whose terraced buildings were once housing for officers who worked in the nearby Dolmabahçe Palace. The Akaretler (www.akaretler.com.tr) houses are now mainly clothing stores, with lots of designer label shops – and this W Hotel. The lively interior – perhaps best summed up as mid-20th century and modern meets Ottoman – has oriental touches among the dark corridors, with flashes of neon. Satiny reds add a gypsyesque touch to the bedrooms, but these are less overtly styled, and are comfortable and modern, with Bose stereos and iPod docks. There is a champagne bar by the lobby, but most of the action happens in the bar upstairs or the restaurant another flight up. With a monthly rotation of international DJs, it is a lively bar that adheres to the W lifestyle ethos of music and fashion. There is also a day spa and café on the premises.

W Istanbul

ESSENTIALS

Getting Around

Arriving & leaving
By air

Istanbul's international **Atatürk Airport** is around 25km (15 miles) west of the city centre in Yeşilköy.

EasyJet and many charter flights arrive at the second international airport, **Sabiha Gökçen**, in Kurtköy on the Asian side. It is 35km (22 miles) from the city centre, but improved transport means it's not the hassle it once was.

Atatürk International Airport
24-hr English flight info 0212 465 3000, www.ataturkairport.com.
Sabiha Gökçen Airport
Kurtköy (0212 585 500 3000, English flight info at www.sgairport.com).

There are three options for getting from the airport to the city centre: bus, light rail underground or taxi. The choice depends on where you're staying and how much time you've got.

The easiest option is with Havaş (0212 444 0487, www.havas.net). Havaş operates the reliable **express airport bus service** from both airports, which leaves for four different destinations from a signposted stop outside the arrivals hall. The only one of use to visitors is the Taksim service – fine if you're staying in Beyoğlu or Taksim – which starts at 4am then runs half-hourly until 11.30pm (4am-midnight to Sabiha Gökçen), stopping en route at the Bakırköy Sea Bus Terminal, Aksaray and Tepebaşı (just short of Taksim). The fare is YTL10 (YTL13 from Sabiha Gökçen), collected by a conductor on board the bus.

The **underground**, or 'light metro', takes you to Aksaray in half an hour and costs just YTL1.50; from here, you can get a bus to Taksim or a tram to Sultanahmet. Services run 6.15am-midnight Mon-Sat, 6.30am-midnight Sun.

Taxis can be taken from the rank outside the arrivals hall. Fares are metered. Journeys to the centre of Sultanahmet should be around YTL18-YTL20 (half as much again at night). The ride takes about 20 minutes but can stretch to 45 minutes if the traffic's bad. To Taksim, it costs around YTL23 and takes anywhere between 20-50 minutes. Taxis from Sabiha Gökçen will be around half as much again.

By rail

Rail travel from the rest of Europe to Istanbul is now the preserve of backpackers and the lower-income end of Turkey's Balkan diaspora.

Trains from Europe arrive at Sirkeci Station (*gar*), beside the Golden Horn in Eminönü. From here, it's a short walk or tram ride up the hill to Sultanahmet. A taxi to Taksim costs YTL5-YTL6.

Trains from destinations to the south and east terminate at Haydarpaşa Station on the Asian shore. Sirkeci and Haydarpaşa stations are connected by ferries. Timetables for international and national services are posted on the state railway (TCDD) website (www.tcdd. gov.tr); the English-language version of the site is refreshingly good.
Sirkeci Station
Istasyon Caddesi, Eminönü (0212 520 6575 ext 417, for reservations 6am-6pm daily).

Haydarpaşa Station
*Haydarpaşa Istasyon Caddesi, Kadıköy
(0216 336 0475, for reservations 6am-
6pm daily).*

By road

Turkish coach companies (such
as Ulusoy and Varan) run regular
services from many European
cities. Be prepared for lengthy
waits at border crossings.

Travellers disembark at the
international and inter-city bus
terminal (*otogar*) in Esenler, about
ten kilometres (six miles) from the
city centre. There are courtesy
minibuses to Taksim and
Sultanahmet. The underground
'light metro' connects the terminal to
Aksaray, where you can trudge to
the Taksim bus stop across the road,
or take a tram to Sultanahmet.

Esenler bus terminal
Uluslararası Istanbul Otogarı
*Büyük Istanbul Otogarı, Bayrampaşa
(0212 658 0505, www.otogar
istanbul.com).* **Open** 24hrs daily.

Ulusoy
*İnönü Caddesi 59, Gümüşsuyu (0212
244 6375/International journeys 0212
658 3006, www.ulusoy.com.tr).* **Open**
24hrs daily.

Varan
*İnönü Caddesi 29/A, Gümüşsuyu (0212
444 8999, www.varan. com.tr).* **Open**
24hrs daily.

Public transport

Public transport is cheap and
improving all the time, thanks
to a municipal campaign to defeat
the city's chronic traffic problem.
Happily, the two areas where
visitors are likely to spend most
time – Beyoğlu and Sultanahmet
– are easily explored on foot.
However, buses are useful
for heading up the Bosphorus
coast. The easiest way to get to
Nişantaşı, Teşvikye, Etiler and

Levent is via the new metro line
that runs north from Taksim.

The informative website of
the IETT (www.iett.gov.tr), the
local transport authority, has an
excellent English version that
includes maps and timetables.

Fares & tickets

Akbil, the 'smart card', is an
electronic travel pass that can be
used on all public transport except
dolmuş and minibuses. You get a
ten per cent discount on fares.
Akbils are available for a small
refundable deposit (YTL6) from
booths at all main bus, sea bus and
metro stations. To use it, firmly
press the circular metal stud into
the socket on the orange machine
located next to the driver on buses,
or to the left of turnstiles at all
metro, light rail, tram and ferry
stations. Recharge at Akbil
machines located at bus, metro
and tram stations, ferry terminals
or Akbil booths.

Particularly useful for visitors is
the *mavi* (blue) travel pass valid for
a day, a week, 15 days or a month.

Metro, trams & Tünel

At present, the metro runs from
Şişhane north to Maslak, stopping
at Taksim, Osmanbey, Şişli,
Gayrettepe, Levent and 4. Levent.
Extensions will take the line south
of Şişhane to the sea bus jetty
at Yenikapı.

The 'light metro' connects
Aksaray (west of the Grand Bazaar)
to the Esenler bus terminal and on
to the airport.

The city's only modern tram
runs from Zeytinburnu via Aksaray,
Sultanahmet, Eminönü by the
Galata Bridge and six more stops
including Karaköy and Kabataş; the
ferry and sea bus terminal. This is a
useful service for visitors, linking

ESSENTIALS

the Grand Bazaar, Haghia Sophia, Sultanahmet, Topkapı, the Egyptian Bazaar and the Golden Horn. You can also use the tram to visit the city walls. Buy tokens from kiosks at tram stops or from nearby shops – the attendant will point you in the right direction) and feed them into the automatic barriers outside the platform. A single trip on the tram costs YTL1.50 irrespective of your destination. The service runs from around 6am-midnight.

A funicular connects Kabataş to Taksim Square, (connecting at the metro).

A 125-year-old funicular, known as the Tünel, ascends from Karaköy to Taksim Square at the southern end of Istiklal Caddesi. The service runs 7am-10pm Mon-Sat and 7.30am-10pm Sun and costs around YTL1. At Tünel, it connects with a century-old tram that shuttles up mile-and-a-half-long Istiklal Caddesi to Taksim Square and back. Akbil can be used for either, but not regular bus tickets. You need to buy a token for the funicular at the entrance, and a ticket for the tram from Tünel Square funicular station or from a vendor in Taksim Square. Tickets for either the tram or funicular cost YTL1.

Buses

Most city buses (*belediye otobüsü*) are operated by the municipality, but there are also private versions (*halk otobüsü*). Municipal buses are red and white or green; all have IETT written on the front. Private ones are pale blue and green, and usually more modern.

Buy tickets (*bilet*) for municipal buses before boarding (they won't take money on the bus). On private buses, pay a conductor seated in the doorway (they will begrudgingly accept coins, but no large bills). Both IETT and private buses accept Akbil (see p151) and charge the same fare (YTL1.50). Tickets for municipal buses are sold from booths at main stops and stations, or newsstands, nearby stalls and itinerant street vendors for a 30 per cent premium.

Newer buses have electronic signboards with route information. Bus stops also have route maps. Still, the sheer number of routes and the interminable traffic and roadworks can make bus travel tricky. Bus services run from 6am to 11pm. Kabataş and Taksim are the two main bus terminals north of the Golden Horn.

Dolmuş & minibuses

A *dolmuş* (which means 'full') is basically a shared taxi that sets off once every seat is taken. *Dolmuş* run fixed routes (starting points and final destinations are displayed in the front window) but with no set stops. Passengers flag the driver down to get on (if there's room) and holler out to be let off (*Inecek var!*). For local journeys, there's one fixed fare (usually YTL1.50). Ask a fellow passenger how much it is or just watch what everyone else is paying. *Dolmuş* run later than buses, often as late as 2am.

Minibuses are more crowded than *dolmuş*, and less frequent. Fares are lower, but chances are you'll make your journey standing while being blasted by tinny Turkish pop. Pay and get on/off as you would a *dolmuş*. The main routes are from Beşiktaş to the upper Bosphorus districts.

Water transport

Timetables are available from ferry terminals; times are also posted online. The main services run between Eminönü, Karaköy,

Kabataş and Beşiktaş on the European side, and Üsküdar and Kadıköy on the Asian shore. Departures are every 15mins or so.

Regular services run up the Golden Horn to Eyüp from Üsküdar via Eminönü. Less frequent commuter services criss-cross the Bosphorus, starting from Eminönü and calling at Haydarpaşa, Ortaköy, Arnavutköy, Bebek, Kandilli and beyond.

The popular Bosphorus tour departs from Eminönü three times daily.

The modern catamarans (*deniz otobüsleri* or 'sea buses') are faster but more expensive and generally restricted to commuter hours.
Istanbul Fast Ferry
Istanbul Deniz Otobüsleri AŞ *Kennedy Caddesi, Sahil Yolu, Hızlı Feribot İskelesi, Yenikapı (0212 444 4436, www.ido.com.tr).*

Taxis

You won't have a problem finding a taxi, day or night. Licensed taxis are bright yellow, with a roof-mounted *taksi* sign. They're all metered, and relatively cheap by European standards. If the meter isn't running, get out.

During the day, the meter displays the word *gündüz* (day rate); the clock should start with YTL2.50. From midnight to 6am the *gece* (night) rate kicks in, adding 50 per cent to the fare. The day rate is YTL1.40 per kilometre. A trip between Sultanahmet and Taksim Square costs YTL6-YTL7. There's no room for haggling and no need to tip. Cabbies are not necessarily streetwise. It's not unusual for your driver to ask you, other drivers or passersby the way. If you cross the Bosphorus bridges, the toll (YTL4) will be added to the fare.

Driving

Driving is not recommended. Heavy congestion doesn't stop speeding, although the limit is 50kmh (30mph), rising to 120kmh (75mph) on motorways. Seat belts are the law, but observance of regulations is laughable.

Car hire

The companies listed below all also have branches at Atatürk airport.
Avis
Abdülhakhamit Caddesi 72/A, off Cumhuriyet Caddesi, Taksim (0212 444 2847, www.avis.com.tr).
Budget
Cumhuriyet Caddesi 19, Taksim (0212 444 4722, www.budget.com.tr).
Europcar
Topçu Caddesi 1/A, off Cumhuriyet Caddesi, Taksim (0212 254 7710, www.europcar.com.tr).

Cycling

Terrible traffic, steep hills, slippery cobbles and countless potholes make Istanbul very challenging for cyclists. However, the wide road alongside the Bosphorus north of Ortaköy is great for biking, with lovely views and a sea breeze. A hired bike is ideal for getting around the Princes' Islands, where cars are banned.

Walking

The tourist hubs of Sultanahmet, the Bazaar Quarter and Beyoğlu are all perfect for exploring on foot (and Beyoğlu's main drag, İstiklal Caddesi, is pedestrianised). There are very few main roads, while the narrow, sloping backstreets are better suited to pedestrians than cars. Pay attention when crossing roads, as drivers often jump lights.

ESSENTIALS

Resources A-Z

Accidents & emergencies

Call the following for the emergency services:
Police 155
Fire 110
Ambulance 112

These hospitals are recommended for emergencies:
American Hospital
Güzelbahçe Sokak 20, Nişantaşı (0212 444 3777, www.amerikan hastanesi.com.tr).
International Hospital
Istanbul Caddesi 82, Yeşilköy (0212 444 0663, www.international hospital.com.tr).
Taksim State Emergency Hospital
Sıraselviler Caddesi 112, Cihangir, Taksim (0212 252 4300).

Credit card loss

American Express
0212 444 2525,
www.americanexpress.com.tr.
Mastercard
00 800 13 887 0903.
Visa
00 800 13 535 0900.

Customs

Foreign visitors can import up to one 100cc (or two 75cc) bottle(s) of alcohol (including wine), 200 cigarettes, 50 cigarillos and ten cigars. You may need proof of purchase for antiques and a carpet. If an item is more than 100 years old there is some red tape that the dealer should help with. For more details, visit www.gumruk.gov.tr or call 0212 465 5244/45.

Dental emergency

The American and International hospitals (see left) have dental clinics.
ADENT Dental Clinic
Çamlık Girişi 6, Etiler (0212 263 1649, www.dentinn.com.tr).
An English-speaking practice.

Disabled

Hilly Istanbul is tough on anyone with a mobility problem. However, public transport is more accessible than before: the new metro has elevators, the light railway and trams are accessible; and some 450 'low-riding' Mercedes buses have been provided to facilitate disabled access. Apart from a handful of top hotels, few buildings make any provisions for the disabled.

Electricity

Electricity in Turkey runs on 220 volts. Plugs have two round pins. Adaptors for UK appliances can be found in hardware shops and on street stalls, but it's still best to bring one from home. Transformers are required for US 110-volt appliances.

Embassies & consulates

All foreign embassies are located in Ankara, but many countries also have a consulate in Istanbul.
Australian Consulate
Askerocağı Caddesi 15, Süzer Plaza 16nd Floor, Şişli (0212 243 1333-36, www.dfat.gov.au). **Open** 8.30am-12.30pm, 1.30-5pm Mon-Fri.

Canadian Consulate
Istiklal Caddesi 189/5, Beyoğlu (0212 251 9838). **Open** 9.30am-12.30pm, 1.30-5.30pm Mon-Thur; 9.30am-12.30pm Fri.

Republic of Ireland Honorary Consulate
Merter İş Merkezi 417, General Ali Rıza Gürcan Caddesi, Merter (0212 482 1862, www.irlconsulist.com). **Open** 9am-5pm Mon-Fri.

New Zealand Honorary Consulate
Inönü Caddesi 48/3, Taksim, Beyoğlu, (0212 244 0272). **Open** 9am-7pm Mon-Fri.

UK Consulate
Meşrutiyet Caddesi 34, Beyoğlu (0212 334 6400, www.fco.gov.uk). **Open** 8.30am-4.45pm Mon-Fri.

US Consulate
Kaplıcalar Mevkii Sokak 2, Istinye Mahallesi, Istinye (0212 335 9000, 340 4444 visas, http://istanbul.us consulate.gov). **Open** 8am-4.30pm Mon-Fri.

Internet

Robin Hood Internet Café
Yeniçarşı Caddesi 8/4, Istiklal Caddesi, Beyoğlu (0212 244 8959). **Open** 9.30am-11pm daily. **Rates** YTL2/hr.

Opening hours

Opening hours vary greatly, but here are some general guidelines:
Banks 9am-12.30pm, 1.30-5pm Mon-Fri.
Museums 8.30am-5.30pm Tue-Sun.
Post offices *see below.*
Shops 10am-8pm Mon-Sat. Local grocery stores and shops in main shopping areas are open until 10pm.

Police

The police emergency number is 155. The main thing to beware of is bag-snatching and pickpocketing.

The police have a reputation for incompetence, excessive use of force, and an appetite for back-handers – which has been generally deserved. Determination to change this image has resulted in a major PR drive: the police website (www.iem.gov.tr) has an exhaustive catalogue of services in ten languages.

Tourist police
Yerebatan Caddesi 6, Sultanahmet (0212 527 4503). Tram Sultanahmet. **Open** 24 hrs daily.
Most officers speak English.

Post

Post offices are recognisable by their yellow and black PTT signs. Stamps can only be bought at post offices.

Beyoğlu
Yeniçarşı Caddesi 4A, Istiklal Caddesi, Beyoğlu (0212 444 1788, www.ptt. gov.tr). **Open** 8.30am-5pm Mon-Fri; 8.30am-7pm Sun.

Sirkeci
Büyük Postane, Büyük Postane Caddesi (0212 444 1788, www.ptt.gov.tr). Tram Sirkeci. **Open** 8.30am-9pm daily.

Taksim
Cumhuriyet Caddesi 2, Beyoğlu (0212 444 1788, www.ptt.gov.tr). **Open** 8.30am-12.30pm, 1.30-5.30pm Mon-Sat.

Smoking

Smoking bans are slowly creeping in: first it was public transport, now it's offices, banks and shops too. Only a few restaurants and cafés offer non-smoking sections.

Telephones

Istanbul's districts have different area codes: 0212 for Europe; 0216 for Asia. You must use the code whenever you call the opposite shore, but when dialling from abroad omit the zero. The country code for Turkey is 90. Call 118 for directory inquiries, 115 for the international operator.

ESSENTIALS

Public phones operate with pre-paid cards (*telefon kartı*). Some newer phones also take credit cards. Phone cards can be bought at post offices or, at a small premium, from street vendors and kiosks.

Local SIM cards (*hazır kart*) are available through all GSM operators. Find an authorised dealer (Turkcell is the most popular), present a photocopy of your passport, and pay the subscription fee (around YTL30-YTL40), which includes 100 units, or roughly 25 minutes of talk-time within Turkey. Top-up cards are sold all over the place.

Time

Turkey is two hours ahead of Greenwich Mean Time (GMT) and seven hours ahead of New York. There is no Turkish equivalent of am and pm, so the 24-hour clock is used. Daylight-saving runs from the last Sunday in March to the last Sunday in October.

Tipping

Although not obligatory, the rule of thumb is to leave about ten per cent of the bill at cafés and restaurants. Service is occasionally included, in which case it'll say *servis dahil* at the bottom of the bill. If in doubt ask: '*Servis dahil mi?*' Tipping hotel staff, porters and hairdressers is discretionary, but YTL1-YTL2 is the norm. Hamam attendants expect more like 25 per cent. It's not necessary to tip taxi drivers.

Tourist information

The Ministry of Culture and Tourism has tourist information kiosks, where staff speak English, all over town.

Atatürk Airport
International Arrivals (0212 465 5555). **Open** 24 hrs daily.

Beyazıt
Beyazıt Square (0212 522 4902). *Tram Beyazıt.* **Open** 9am-6pm daily.

Hilton Hotel
Cumhuriyet Caddesi, Şişli (0212 233 0592). **Open** 9am-5pm daily.

Karaköy Seaport
Kemankeş Caddesi, Karaköy (0212 249 5776). Tram Karaköy. **Open** 9am-5pm Mon-Sat.

Sirkeci Station
Istasyon Caddesi, Sirkeci. Tram Sirkeci (0212 511 5888). **Open** 9am-5pm daily.

Sultanahmet Square
Divan Yolu 3 (0212 518 1802). Tram Sultanahmet. **Open** 9am-5pm daily.

Visas & immigration

Visas are required by most nationalities; they can be bought at the airport upon arrival. At press time, rates are as follows: UK $20; USA $20; Canada $60; Australia $20; Ireland $20. New Zealanders don't need a visa. Fees must be paid in euros or dollars. UK passport holders can pay £10 in sterling; Turkish lira, credit cards or travellers' cheques are not accepted. Visas are valid for three months. Overstaying your visa, even by a single day, will earn you a fine of around YTL150 ($100) when you finally leave the country.

If you have a work permit, you're automatically entitled to residence as long as your permit is valid. Otherwise, residence applications should be filed with the Turkish Consulate General in your country of residence. The laborious application procedure for British passport holders is detailed online at www.turkconsulate-london.com.

What's on

Time Out Istanbul magazine (www.timeout.com/istanbul), covers events, restaurants, bars, arts and nightlife.

Vocabulary

Pronunciation

All words are written phonetically and except ğ there are no silent letters; so post office, *postane*, is pronounced 'post-a-neh'. Syllables are articulated with equal stress. The key is to master the pronunciation of the few letters and vowels that differ from English:

c – like the 'j' in jam; so cami (mosque) is 'jami'
ç – like the 'ch' in chip, so çiçek (flower) is 'chi-check'
ğ – silent, but lengthens preceding vowel
ı – an 'uh', like the 'a' in cinema
ö – like the 'ir' in girdle
ş – like the 'sh' in shop, so şiş (as in kebab) is pronounced 'shish'
ü – as in the French 'tu'

Accommodation

air-conditioning klima; **bathroom** banyo; **bed** yatak; **bed & breakfast** pansiyon; **breakfast** kahvaltı; **double bed** çift kişilik yatak; **hotel** otel; **no vacancies** yer yok; **room** oda; **shower** duş; **soap** sabun; **towel** havlu; **vacancy** yer var.

Essentials

a lot/very/too çok; **and** ve; **bad/ badly** kötü; **big** büyük; **but** ama/ fakat; **good/well** iyi; **I don't speak Turkish** Türkçe bilmiyorum; **I don't understand** anlayamadım; **leave me alone** (quite forceful) beni rahat bırak; **Mr/Mrs** bey/ hanım (with first name); **no** hayır; **OK** tamam; **please** lütfen; **small** küçük; **sorry** pardon; **thank you** teşekkürler/mersi/sağol; **yes** evet; **this/that** bu/şu;

Getting around

airport havalimanı; **bus** otobüs; **bus/coach station** otogar; **car park** otopark; **entrance** giriş; **exit** çıkış; **left** sol; **map** harita; **platform** peron; **road** yol; **station** gar; **street** sokak; **train** tren.

Greetings

good morning günaydın; **good afternoon/goodbye** iyi günler; **good evening/goodbye** iyi akşamlar; **good night/goodbye** iyi geceler; **goodbye** güle güle (to the person leaving); **hello** merhaba;

Questions

do you have change? bozuk paranız var mı? **do you speak English?** ingilizce biliyor musunuz? **how?** nasıl? **how many?** kaç tane? **how much (price)?** kaç para? **what?** ne? **when?** ne zaman? **where?** nerede? **where to?** nereye? **which (one)?** hangi(si)? **who?** kim? **why?** niye/niçin/neden?

Sightseeing

castle kale; **church** kilise; **closed** kapalı; **free** bedava/ücretsiz; **open** açık; **mosque** cami; **museum** müze; **palace** saray; **reduced price** indirimli; **ticket** bilet.

Numbers

0 sıfır; **1** bir; **2** iki; **3** üç; **4** dört; **5** beş; **6** altı; **7** yedi; **8** sekiz; **9** dokuz; **10** on; **11** onbir; **12** oniki; **20** yirmi; **21** yirmibir; **22** yirmiiki; **30** otuz; **40** kırk; **50** elli; **60** altmış; **70** yetmiş; **80** seksen; **90** doksan; **100** yüz; **1,000** bin.

Index

ESSENTIALS